PROFESSIONAL DEVELOPMENT SERIES

I. MPROVE
M. ANAGEMENT
E. FFECTIVENESS

A Practical Approach To Managerial Time

George R. Carnahan
Northern Michigan University

Brian G. Gnauck
Northern Michigan University

David B. Hoffman
University of Alaska

Bruce C. Sherony
Northern Michigan University

U05

Published by

SOUTH-WESTERN PUBLISHING CO.

CINCINNATI WEST CHICAGO, IL DALLAS LIVERMORE, CA

ISBN: 0-538-21050-8

Library of Congress Catalog Card Number: 85-63629

1 2 3 4 5 6 7 8 9 E 4 3 2 1 0 9 8 7 6

Printed in the United States of America

Preface

8:45 P.M.
November 16

As Ron Holland pulls into his driveway, he realizes that the sun set several hours ago. He's just arriving home from his industrial supply business, and it's 8:45 in the evening. There were just too many distractions and meetings and too much paperwork to get away sooner. His youngest son is getting ready for bed, and once again his dinner will be a cold sandwich.

He drives into the garage and turns off the engine but remains in the car thinking how frustrated he feels. He wanted to be home earlier, but he had a lot of work to do. If he hadn't tackled the work today, it would have been buried under tomorrow's demands.

> It seems the only way to get more done in the day is to stay at the office until it's finished. There has to be a better way! Starting tomorrow, I'm going to keep a record of what I do all day and start managing my time so that I use it more effectively. If the only way to get more done is to stay at work longer, then I'm at the end of my rope. I know there are some differences between what I'm doing now and what I need to be doing. It sure would be nice to get the job done and still get home to have dinner with my family.

Ron gets out of the car and closes the garage door. He already feels better as he walks into the house. He is finally going to take charge of the situation.

Does any part of this story have a familiar ring? The frustration, the late evenings, or the fact that work piles up at an uncontrollable rate? A manager's success depends on a variety of factors, including education, training, experience, and, to a great extent, the problems to be solved, the resources available, and other conditions that influence the day's activities.

The challenge for any manager is not only to improve personal performance but ultimately to improve the performance of the organization. This is never an easy task, and, as anyone will admit, work seems to demand a great deal of time. The management of one's time and activities thus becomes an important part of the overall management process.

Ron Holland's situation is common but not necessary. We will use Ron and three other managers to demonstrate the use of some specific strategies for handling the relentless war of time and demands. As we evaluate their situations, analyzing the problems and suggesting possible solutions, we introduce a framework for understanding and improving management effectiveness: the T.I.M.E. (To Improve Management Effectiveness) model. This model represents a practical approach to the use of managerial time.

Chapter 2 presents a traditional approach to the subject of managerial time: a review of time wasters that are common to a broad range of managerial positions. Chapter 3 covers in detail the T.I.M.E. model: a precise description of the model's components, including environment, experience, individual characteristics, awareness, action, and improved performance. Chapter 4 examines the model's dimensions and relationships.

Chapter 5 uses the model to classify time wasters, placing the misuses of managerial time in a performance mode. Chapter 6 shows how to develop awareness of misuses of managerial time by use of the Daily T.I.M.E. Record. Chapter 7 gives precise directions on how individual managers take appropriate action by reviewing major T.I.M.E. Tactics. Chapter 8 concludes with a demonstration of how the T.I.M.E. model results in improved performance, showing techniques and mechanisms for measuring that performance.

This book, therefore, provides a practical approach to the misuse of managerial time and the quest for improved management effectiveness. At this point we invite you to turn the page and join us as we learn about the events that affected Ron Holland on November 16 and the T.I.M.E. seminar that followed.

Contents

List of Figures

1

TWO DAYS IN THE LIFE OF RON HOLLAND

6:30 A.M.
November 16

Ron awakes at 6:30 A.M. Thoughts pass through his mind: What's on the schedule today at work? Issues and problems are mentally enumerated in a random fashion: customer complaints, deer season, employee absences, and sales force meetings.

Ron's regional industrial supply business is only twenty minutes from his home. He arrives at 7:45 A.M. The digital clock on the wall turns to 8:00, and Jim Sheard arrives. Jim is one of four district sales managers for Ron's supply business. Jim reacts to Ron's presence by saying, "What did you think of the Miami Dolphins--Dallas Cowboys football game last night?" Ron responds, "I didn't get a chance to see it, but I understand it was a great game." For a few moments the conversation focuses on the football season and the most recent games.

It is now 8:16 and the telephone rings. Ron's secretary has not yet arrived, so he picks up the phone. Quickly he refers the call to Jim Sheard, since the matter is a complaint of a customer in his territory.

At 8:30 Ron starts a monthly sales meeting with his four district sales managers, during which the managers report the status of selling in their territories, update him on significant new prospects, and summarize sales activities by major product category.

The meeting concludes at 10:01. Ron leaves the conference room and enters his office. Gloria Alvarez, manager of warehouse and inventory, is waiting for him. Ron is confused. He finally realizes that he and Gloria had scheduled a meeting for 9:30 that morning. Ron shuffles through a stack of papers to find the matter he wanted to discuss with Gloria. His secretary assists, and together they locate the material. Miss Alvarez informs Ron that two men are absent from the warehouse and that she suspects they are deer hunting. Ron tells Gloria to handle it. The other items are covered quickly.

The time is now 10:30, and Ron Holland leaves his office to get a cup of coffee. He returns to his office and begins fumbling through a stack of papers and pamphlets on his desk. Certain items need immediate action, and one in particular catches his attention: an issue that relates to a new employee fringe benefit package he is considering. He begins to read it, then sets it down and continues reviewing the papers in front of him.

A supplier of an innovative warehousing rack system telephones. Ron has talked with the supplier before and wants to obtain more information about the system. His secretary interrupts: "Another call." "Who's on the line?" Ron responds. "It's a customer from Jim Sheard's district who needs to speak to you," she states. Ron quickly concludes his conversation with the rack salesman and takes the call. The customer is concerned about an order that has not arrived and is curious to know when it was shipped. Ron talks with the customer for a few minutes and assures him that Jim Sheard will contact him immediately. He hangs up and calls Jim.

The time is now 11:30 A.M., and Ron's coffee is cold. He realizes that he needs to leave for his noon luncheon meeting with a potential industrial account. Ron usually handles the large industrial accounts himself as these are considered "house accounts," not part of the district territory sales clientele.

Ron leaves the building, grabbing his coat and the papers he needs for his meeting. He has a twenty-minute drive across town and arrives at the prearranged location to meet Michi Komuro. Ron's interaction with Mrs. Komuro goes smoothly. His friendly personality, communication skills, and ability to employ his engineering background are key attributes that help him obtain Mrs. Komuro's business. This is a major account, and Ron is pleased with the results of the meeting. Komuro and Holland leave the restaurant at 1:15 P.M.

Arriving back at the office, Ron is immediately met by his secretary, who has a list of four telephone calls and memos that she brings to his attention. He needs to call Sarah Lute, an inspector from OSHA who stopped by the warehouse. There is also a message to call Eric Mead, a long-time friend. Ron and Eric enjoy playing golf whenever possible. He also received telephone calls from Alan Specker, a salesperson who has contacted him frequently about physical handling for his warehouse, and from Becky Thomas, who requested that Ron return her call. Ms. Thomas is a young college graduate with a degree in marketing who has approached Ron about securing a job in sales. Ron has known Becky's father for many years and has watched Becky grow up.

Ron picks up the telephone and calls Eric. Eric answers and Ron says, "Hi, Eric." Eric, obviously recognizing Ron's voice, responds, "How's it going?" In a loud, boisterous voice, Ron replies, "Good—what's up?" "How about a last round of golf for the year?" suggests Eric. Ron pauses for a moment as he mulls over the various things he has to do. "Well, maybe we can work it in on Friday. No—can't make it on Friday. Let's make it—what are you doing Saturday?" Eric responds, "I'll see you at seven o'clock at the first tee." The joking conversation continues for another ten minutes. Finally, Ron concludes, "I have to get back to business."

It is now 2 P.M. and Ron is determined to get the stack of papers off his desk. He sets his telephone calls aside and continues to review the paperwork. One item draws his attention. Large, bold letters on a color brochure state *T.I.M.E. To Improve Management Effectiveness: A Practical Approach to Managerial Time.* He opens the brochure, begins to read, and soon realizes that the seminar may be of value. It is scheduled for November 26, in Minneapolis. He realizes that he can get a plane connection to arrive in Minneapolis at 9 A.M. He should be able to make it to the Holiday Inn by the 9:30 A.M. starting time. He calls his secretary and tells her to make a reservation for him.

Ron finishes stacking the paperwork in three piles: (1) primarily junk mail, (2) high-priority materials he wants to deal with that day or in the very near future, and (3) issues that can be delayed. Ron discards the junk mail and starts to attack the priority stack.

The first item he reviews is a study by Gloria Alvarez of fuel consumption in the warehouse. Ron finishes reading the report and looks up; it is 3:30. His afternoon replicates the earlier part of his day. We already know that he won't arrive home until 8:45 P.M.

Ron Holland's activities on the workdays before Thanksgiving were pretty much a duplication of November 16. His inability to organize his day, and to identify, categorize, and understand classic time wasters reduced his overall managerial performance.

Thanksgiving came, and Ron had an enjoyable time with his family, including his daughter, who had returned from college. On November 26 he headed for the T.I.M.E. seminar. He left for the airport at 6:30 A.M. and had an uneventful flight to Minneapolis. Upon arrival, he took a cab to the hotel and then proceeded to the Voyagers' Room, the location for the T.I.M.E. seminar.

Ron Holland entered the room and proceeded to the coffee table. The tall man ahead of him in line introduced himself as Bob Koski, from the Homer Corporation in Minneapolis. When Ron asked what position he held, Bob responded that he was a corporate controller. Ron learned that the Homer Corporation was one of the *Fortune* 500 and that Bob had been with the company for twenty-five years. He had an undergraduate degree in business administration from Purdue University and a number of years back had received his Master of Business Administration degree from the University of Minnesota. He was fifty-two years old and seemed to be quite settled in his current position.

Ron and Bob continued conversation for a number of minutes. Ron Holland was impressed by one thing that Bob Koski had said. He paraphrased it in his mind:

> Even though you think you are an efficient and effective manager, it is sometimes surprising how marginal improvements in the use of time can make marked improvement in your overall managerial performance and make your life easier.

Ron and Bob found two vacant chairs at a table occupied by Jeff Med and Christina Jones. Jeff Med was assistant plant manager of St. Martin's Paper Company, a local pulp and paper manufacturer. Jeff had been in the position for five years and had recently completed a master's degree in paper chemistry from a Wisconsin university. He was responsible for assisting the plant manager in a broad array of activities. The plant was structured around 450 production personnel, and overall employment at the location was about 550 people. Jeff Med's job had a classic production orientation: production schedules, quality control, inventory control, and the personnel problems that arise in a modern production facility. Jeff was very cognizant of time, since the production facility was running on a three-shift basis.

Christina Jones was the office manager for Security Mutual Insurance Company. Ron asked Christina why she was participating in a time management seminar. She responded:

> "I was curious to find out if the way I work makes sense or if there are ways in which I can improve my use of time. At times I seem to be extremely pressed to accomplish all my assigned tasks. I'm responsible for managing forty staff personnel, including secretaries, clerks, and actuaries. We run a one-shift operation and are structured in open modules on the thirty-first floor of the company offices."

The clock was moving toward 9:30 A.M., time for the seminar to begin. Ron Holland, Bob Koski, Jeff Med, Christina Jones, and about forty-five other participants sat back to listen.

2
MISUSE OF MANAGERIAL TIME: TIME WASTERS

9:30 A.M.
November 26

To discuss the problem of managerial time, we must first look at the traditional time wasters. You must answer two simple questions: How do you misuse your time? What causes you to waste time? On the form in Figure 2-1, list what you believe are the ways you waste time, then you can compare your list with comments by some seminar participants.

> Christina Jones commented, "Too much visiting takes place because our offices are wide open." Jeff Med interjected, "I think the telephone is a big waster of time," and others agreed with him. Other participants suggested a poor filing system and the general workload. After about ten minutes, many different time wasters had been mentioned.

It is interesting that when asked to name their time wasters, most people mentioned the same factors. A considerable amount of research has been done in this area. If you compare your listing in Figure 2-1 (and the comments of the seminar participants) to the list in Figure 2-2, you will probably see more similarities than differences.

It's important that the task of identifying time wasters not stop at this point. You should continue working on your list, even though it may take some time. By identifying misuses of time, you are in a position to start correcting these abuses.

> Bob Koski asked a question at this point in the seminar: "How does a list like this help me to be a better manager? I know that in my case, meetings are a time waster, but I have little or no control over many of these meetings."

This is a good question, and it is why our approach to managerial

Figure 2-1 Time Wasters Worksheet

Time Wasters

Name ____________________ Job Title ____________________

1. ______________________________
2. ______________________________
3. ______________________________
4. ______________________________
5. ______________________________
6. ______________________________
7. ______________________________
8. ______________________________
9. ______________________________
10. ______________________________
11. ______________________________
12. ______________________________
13. ______________________________
14. ______________________________
15. ______________________________
16. ______________________________
17. ______________________________
18. ______________________________
19. ______________________________
20. ______________________________

Figure 2-2 The Fourteen Major Misuses of Managerial Time

Major Time Wasters

1. Telephone interruptions
2. Drop-in visitors
3. Misused meetings
4. Crisis management
5. Lack of objectives, priorities, and daily plan
6. Cluttered desk / personal disorganization
7. Ineffective delegation of responsibilities
8. Attempting too much at once
9. Insufficient and unclear communications
10. Indecision
11. Procrastination
12. Inability to say no
13. Leaving tasks unfinished
14. Lack of self-discipline

Adapted from R. Alec MacKenzie, *The Time Trap: How To Get More Done in Less Time,* (New York: McGraw-Hill, 1972) page 6.

time uses the T.I.M.E. model. Traditional approaches to time management generally leave you with a list, which becomes difficult to apply to change your use of managerial time once you are on the job. In other words, the traditional approach does not place the question of time use into a performance mode or perspective.

In the special setting of a seminar it is relatively easy to identify how we, as individual managers, misuse our time. However, a review of traditional time wasters will not necessarily change bad habits. You also need a plan by which wasted time can be categorized. Once you understand how time wasters pervade your day and affect how much you can accomplish, you are in a better position to correct your misuses of time. You can then achieve your ultimate goal – To Improve Management Effectiveness.

This book therefore introduces the T.I.M.E. model. The model is not complex, but it does include a number of components and dimensions. These will be introduced one at a time in the next two chapters.

3

THE T.I.M.E. MODEL: TO IMPROVE MANAGEMENT EFFECTIVENESS

10 A.M.
November 26

The job performance of any manager depends on such factors as previous education, training, and experience, as well as a number of work-related factors. The challenge inherent in any time management program is not only the improvement of one's managerial skills but ultimately the improvement of organizational performance.

In order for both of these goals to be achieved, people will have to change existing patterns of thought and behavior—not an easy task because habits have been acquired over a long time. Also, the nature and magnitude of the desire to change varies from individual to individual. In this context, the management of time becomes an important part of the overall management process. With the information presented here, we hope to provide a means for anyone to use time more effectively, and, by doing so, To Improve Management Effectiveness (T.I.M.E.).

The most effective way to improve management effectiveness is not by simply reviewing classic time wasters. Certainly these have a place in understanding and improving overall management effectiveness, but they don't get at the root causes of the misuse of time. For this we need the T.I.M.E. model.

The model represents a comprehensive set of components that aid a manager in achieving improved performance. Understanding the model involves analyzing each component and then studying the relationship among components. This chapter focuses on the meaning of the various components and the relationship of the components to each other and to the manager. The dimensions of the T.I.M.E. model are discussed in Chapter 4.

Components of the T.I.M.E. Model

The following components comprise the basic properties of the T.I.M.E. model:

1. Environment
2. Experience
3. Individual Characteristics
4. Awareness
5. Action
6. Improved Performance

Component 1: Environment

Many problems that managers face result from factors in their environment. The term ***environment*** refers to several things. First, it refers to *the immediate work setting*—that is, desks, telephones, furniture, customers, equipment, buildings, and money. During a typical day, these resources and physical facilities all affect how we use our time. Before we can be better users of time, we must understand the immediate work setting in which we use time.

A second factor of the work environment is the *general organization conditions* in which we execute work activities. A canceled order is a lost opportunity. The absence of key personnel will slow down the execution of tasks within a production facility or a sales organization. The general organizational conditions that make up the environment can vary from the degree of noise, dust, smoke, and vibration in the plant facility to the quiet tension that pervades a meeting of the board of directors.

A third factor that makes up the environment is the *nature of the people* with whom we work. An individual manager's overall effectiveness depends on how well he or she knows and works with the people above and below him or her. The process of delegation works only if subordinates have the capability to take on the tasks delegated to them. The sources of information and knowledge—upper levels of management—become more effective if good channels of communication are available through which information can flow from top-level management to employees on the lower levels. The use of time, therefore, is very much keyed to the character of the people who surround us every day.

Ron Holland's mind was working double-time as he listened to the presentation. He started to think about his immediate work setting, both the general organizational conditions of the company and the nature of the people. He thought about his desk and office setting. His desk was always filled with paper. Sometimes he could not get to his phone. As he thought further he realized that his furniture was not arranged in the best format for ease of entry and exit. Slowly but surely, as he reflected on these environmental factors and applied them to his business, he started to understand that environment is one of the first components that affects how we use time.

Another factor of the environment is our *family, friends, and culture.* Family, friends, and cultural background influence how we use time. For example, a person who is married and has a family may sometimes need to direct time and energy away from immediate work objectives and toward family objectives. How managers balance these opposing responsibilities and pressures is affected by the values of their culture and the expectations of the people close to them.

A fifth factor of the environment is *climate and weather.* The overall climate and weather can influence time use in a broad sense, and specific weather problems can directly interrupt production processes, deliveries, and other business activities. Just ask anyone who works for a lumber company, public utility, delivery service, or airline. In many jobs climate and weather significantly influence how we allocate time in the short run.

The last factor in our environment that we will discuss is *mass media.* The mass media today bring enormous amounts of information to us at incredible speeds: Local, national, and international news events are known to us seconds after they occur. The speed with which information, data, new technology, and other innovations are brought to our attention is increasing year by year. This availability of more knowledge significantly influences the environment in which we live.

We must also recognize that our environment constantly changes. As a simple example we can all appreciate, reflect on how the environment of the administrative assistant or senior secretary has changed with the development and application of word processing facilities over the last three years.

We can summarize by saying that the environment, the first component of our model, includes the immediate work setting; the general organizational conditions within which we work; the nature of the people with whom we work; the character of family, friends, and our cultural background; the climate and weather; and the mass media. Figure 3-1 summarizes these factors.

Figure 3-1 Factors That Determine the Component Called Environment

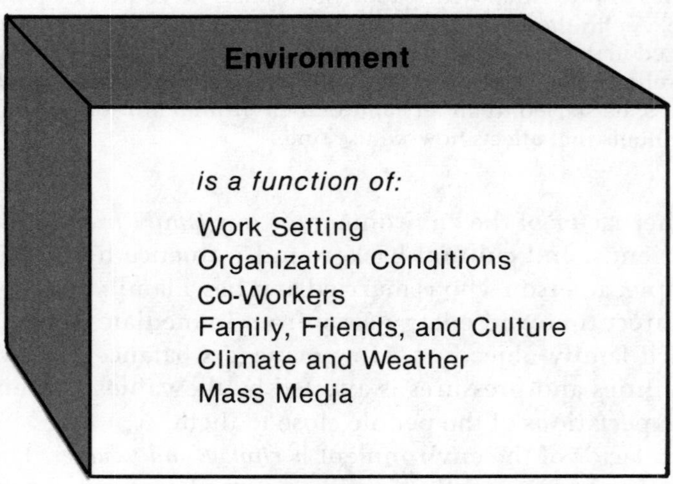

T.I.M.E. Component
Environment
is a function of:
Work Setting
Organization Conditions
Co-Workers
Family, Friends, and Culture
Climate and Weather
Mass Media

Component 2: Experience

> "Why did she get the promotion and I fail to get it?" His boss answered, "Because she had five years of experience, and all you have is one year of experience five times."

We are creatures of memory, and we have the unique ability to anticipate. Our skills enable us to project into the future based on our past. We learn to develop mental heuristics (rules of thumb) from which we act as we live, watch, try, learn, and evaluate. A person who journeys to the same place a second time does certain things differently because of what he or she learned from the first journey; the second journey is better planned. A third journey would probably go even more smoothly because of the increased experience. Eventually, we may even start experimenting as we develop. This experimentation may broaden our experience more than simple repetition, and it may also lead to a new learning experience that was not possible before. The relationship illustrated in Figure 3-2 helps define the factors that make up our ***experience***.

Experience is more than knowledge; it is knowledge applied. Application of knowledge can lead to more effective utilization of time. People who have worked a number of years or who have done a variety of things in and outside of work generally have broader knowledge, which

Figure 3-2 Factors That Determine the Component Called Experience

T.I.M.E. Component

Experience

is a function of the:

Number of Years of Work
Variety of Work
Degree of Responsibility
Number of Years of Training
Number of Years of Formal Education
Variety of Subjects That Were Studied
Diversity of Non-Job Activities

often enhances their effectiveness, sometimes in unexpected ways. Take, for example, a personnel director who was involved in a critical phase of collective bargaining. A great deal of tension had been created and a strong adversarial relationship had evolved during this phase of the bargaining process. To help the parties come to agreement on a particular issue, the negotiator needed to break the tension, which he did with a humorous reference to a literary work. Both bargaining parties softened their stands and were able to reach an agreement more quickly. This manager was able to make the literary reference because of his interest in reading in his leisure time. This broader interest, even though it was not job-related, resulted in more effective use of time at work.

The nature of your experience will provide a basis for understanding how you use time and will help you determine how to improve your use of time. Thus, all of these factors — years and variety of responsibility, amount of training, type of training, education, and nonjob activities — can influence how you use time.

Component 3: Individual Characteristics

Managers approach problems differently because of their individual differences. One source of differences in managerial styles results from differences in attitudes. An *attitude* is a mental position with regard to or a feeling toward a fact. Taken together, the manager's *attitudes* are his or her pattern of belief. Attitudes are acquired through experience, consciously or unconsciously. The degree of intensity of an attitude can range from very strong to almost nonexistent, and the direction can be either positive or negative. Attitudes allow us to act quickly, without reconsidering all the facts every time we must make a decision.

For example, one manager has a very important task to accomplish, so she delegates it to one of her most competent subordinates to increase the chances of completing it satisfactorily. This manager's decision was based on attitudes that had evolved over time – attitudes that classified subordinates as highly effective, moderately effective, and so on. These attitudes may have been based on objective evaluations as well as on more subjective definitions of effectiveness and competency. A large variety of impressions formulate the attitudes in the manager's memory about her subordinates' competence, and effectiveness.

Motivation is the degree of energy that is mobilized and exerted when action takes place. The motive directing the energy should be stated as a goal and should be related to the needs of those employees participating in the achievement of the goal.

Figure 3-3 Factors That Determine the Component Called Individual Characteristics

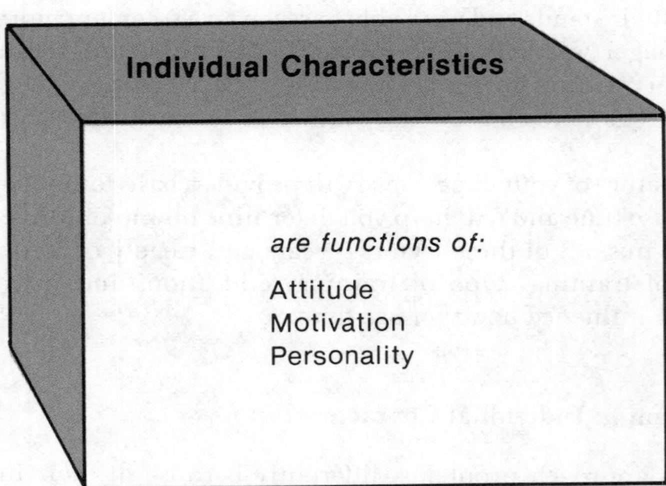
T.I.M.E. Component
Individual Characteristics
are functions of:
Attitude
Motivation
Personality

During a performance review, for example, a supervisor may inform a subordinate that if the subordinate would increase his effort by a certain amount, certain goals of the company would likely be achieved and would be documented in a future evaluation (recognized performance). Further, if such goals were achieved, the subordinate would be rewarded accordingly (need satisfaction).

Personality is the sum of all behaviors that define who we are. Certain traits are helpful for managers or subordinates; others can hinder us as we perform our duties. The subordinate who has an abrasive personality and who angers other subordinates may eventually be dismissed from a job or become an isolate. Such a personality may appear to be "too strong" for the required context of the work environment.

Knowledge of attitudes, motivation, and personality will help you understand ***individual characteristics*** and utilize time. Figure 3-3 illustrates this concept.

Component 4: Awareness

Awareness is related to both realization and alertness (see Figure 3-4). Think about how our past and present environment makes us aware of

Figure 3-4 Factors That Determine the Component Called Awareness

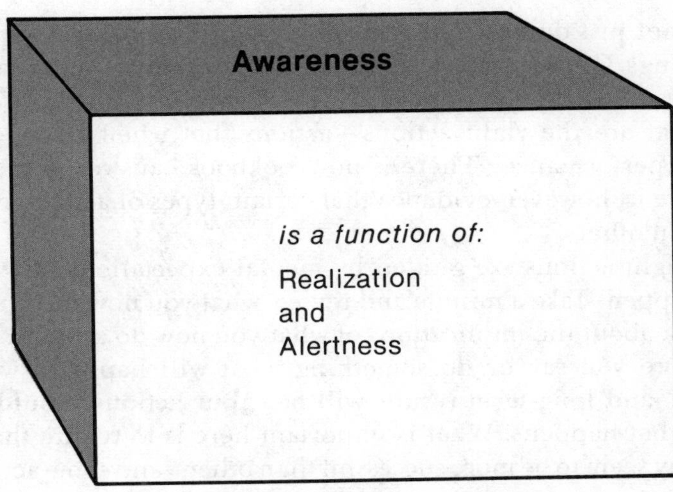
T.I.M.E. Component
Awareness
is a function of:
Realization
and
Alertness

what's around us. We store information within ourselves. This information comes from our senses — from our ability to hear, see, talk, smell, and feel. The information we receive is continually being updated as more information comes to us through our senses. If the new information corresponds with the information already stored, our ideas are supported; and we are encouraged to take certain, hopefully appropriate, actions.

The fact that you are reading this book indicates an awareness on your part. You realized that something was not right, that you needed some assistance in managing your time, and that you needed to improve your performance on the job. You were alert to the possibility of assistance and, consequently, alert to this book when it came to your attention. If you had not realized that there was a problem and had not been alert to ways of solving it, you would not be reading this book.

If the information we encounter doesn't fit our previous beliefs, clarification is required by another party or by our own reasoning. Cohesive feelings are required to take action. We can't take appropriate action when we face confusing and contradictory information.

The relationship of awareness to good job performance is a little difficult to grasp at first. The main concept to remember is that we cannot take appropriate action until we are aware of those factors that affect our choice of action. It is part of our job to see that we become aware. We should also remember that in dealing with subordinates, we must make them as aware as possible of those factors that will affect their performance on the job. This is one way to become a better manager.

Component 5: Action

Action is not just doing and saying things; it is doing and saying the correct things. Our concern is not the amount of activity but the achievement of results. And that's not easy.

So what are the right actions — actions that when taken, achieve improved performance? There is no "cookbook" answer to that question. There is, however, evidence that certain types of action get better results than others.

The right actions are guided by mental expectations of what you want to happen. Take a minute and review what you now do during the day. Think about the implications of what you now do at work. Do you know before you say or do something what will happen — what the immediate and long-term results will be? Your actions should be the cause of what happens. What is important here is to realize that some actions may seem to be more successful than others, and some actions are a waste of time. Rather than trying to identify specific actions, such as conducting a meeting, classify each action in terms of the degree to which it leads to improved performance. Use the factors that make up this component, as listed in Figure 3-5.

Figure 3-5 Activities That Determine the Component Called Action

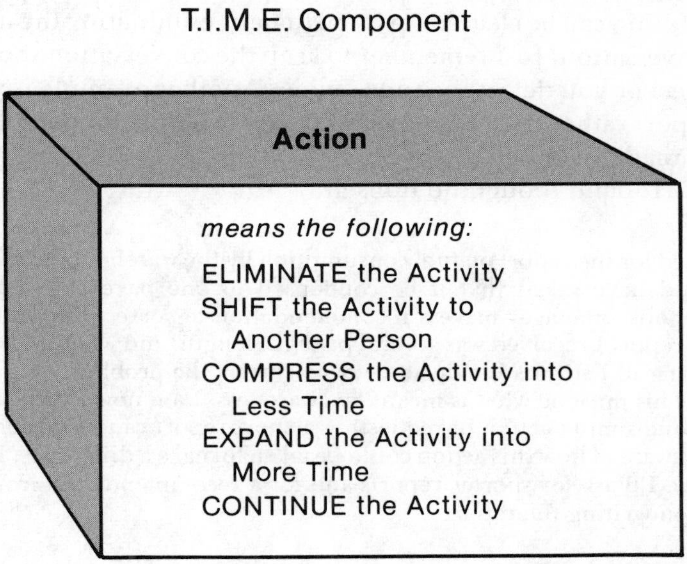

T.I.M.E. Component

Action

means the following:

ELIMINATE the Activity
SHIFT the Activity to Another Person
COMPRESS the Activity into Less Time
EXPAND the Activity into More Time
CONTINUE the Activity

Eliminating the activity refers to activities that do not help improve performance, either yours or the organization's. These activities are, for the most part, time wasters. They neither help get the work done nor in any way provide motivation or job-related rewards for yourself or others. The elimination of activities is sometimes difficult because some of the actions that fit into this category include personal inefficiencies that have become a comfortable part of your work day. An example would be reading the morning paper while having your first cup of coffee at the office in the morning. Maybe you could review something else while having that coffee.

Shifting the activity to another person, the intentional transfer of activities to someone else, is often overlooked. Ron Holland thought for a moment:

> I did this with the problem of the two employees who took the day off to go deer hunting. I told the warehouse manager to handle it.

Even if the other people are not as skilled as you are in performing a task, by assigning the activity to them, you give them the opportunity to learn, and you are given a little more independence. You may have to provide some guidance and spend more time in the short run, but in the long run you both may benefit.

Compressing activities, expanding activities, and *continuing activities* are usually the greatest sources for improving performance. Many tactics for managing time fall into these categories. For example, instead of writing a note, call the person on the telephone. It is not only faster but any confusion can be cleared up immediately, eliminating the need for a later conversation. Just remember to keep the conversation short and to the subject or you defeat the time saving. Another example is writing a short report rather than a long one. It takes less time for both the writer and the reader.

Ron Holland thought to himself:

> I asked for the report on fuel consumption by the warehouse forklifts. I should have asked that it be condensed to one page and that the warehouse manager make a recommendation to correct the problem. The report I received was several pages in length, and when I finished reading it, I still had to decide how to correct the problem.
>
> This must be what is meant by awareness. I am now aware of how this one simple action of requesting a short report can save time. I'm now aware of how this action could be taken to make a difference. In the future I'll ask for shorter reports and for a recommendation from the person writing the report.

Expanding activities means devoting more time to doing certain things. This also means doing some things more carefully because greater care now may save time later. Actions such as thinking, problem solving, planning, and listening fall into this category. Since you have eliminated, shifted, and compressed other activities, you should find that you have more time to do a quality job on those tasks that really make a difference.

Continuing activities means that you continue doing some activities as you always have. These actions are already being appropriately performed and need to be continued.

Action leads to action. By making assignments, making commitments, meeting schedules, and a thousand other things, we cause ourselves and others to move toward future actions. That is useful if the additional actions also lead to desired results. For example, if a meeting leads to scheduling a future meeting at which everyone will be prepared to make a decision, the second meeting will eliminate the need for a third, fifth, or tenth meeting. President Franklin Roosevelt is reported to have said: "But above all, try something." Always, the important point is getting results.

Component 6: Improved Performance

By ***improved performance*** we mean improved organizational performance, which results from improved performance of individuals within the organization. We all perform at some level, and as managers, our performance is based both on what we accomplish and on the accomplishments of those who work with us and for us.

Performance can have many meanings. In terms of efficiency, it can refer to output compared to input—for example, the number of orders taken compared to the number of sales calls in a given day. This is measuring how much is accomplished given a particular amount of effort. An efficient organization accomplishes more with less effort.

Another term associated with performance is *effectiveness,* which refers to the degree of goal achievement (not just any goals but appropriate goals). This is a valuable concept because an effective organization is a collection of individuals who are achieving useful goals in a timely manner.

Figure 3-6 Factors That Measure the Component Called Improved Performance

T.I.M.E. Component
Improved Performance
relates to:
Productivity
Effectiveness
Goal Achievement
Market Share
Sales Growth

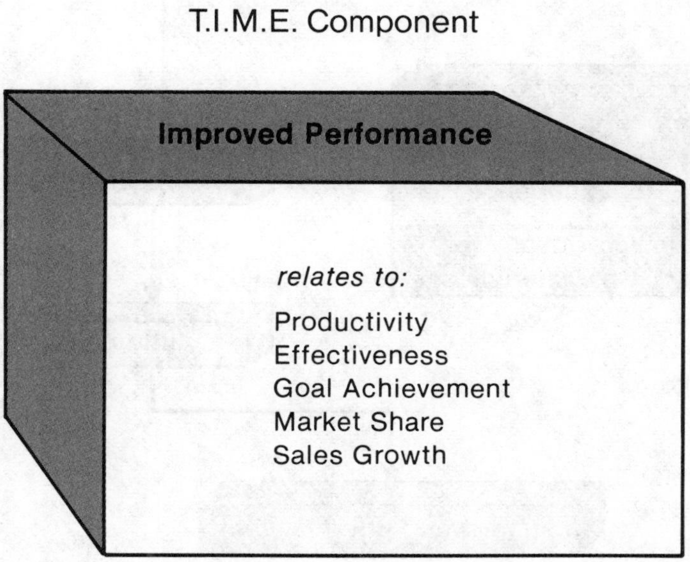

Other measures that are used to gauge performance include profitability, market share, and sales. These are useful because they represent some aspect of the performance of the organization.

There are always subjective considerations to defining performance. These factors should not be abandoned. If you determine, for example, that the morale of the employees should be enhanced, individual efforts to improve morale should be considered even if the results are not quantifiable.

After looking at Figure 3-6, take a few minutes to think about ways to improve your performance. Allow your thoughts to recognize that performance can relate to many different aspects of your own business. Try to identify these aspects of your business that relate to performance. Keep in mind those factors in your company — they can be either quantitative or qualitative in nature — and relate them to your own and your subordinates' performance.

Component Relationships

At this point, you should have a clear understanding of the T.I.M.E.

Figure 3-7 General Relationship Among the Six Components of the T.I.M.E. Model

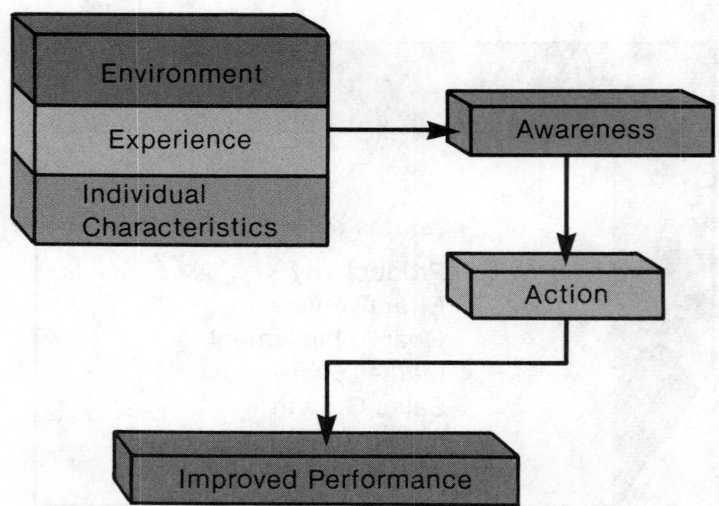

components. We now present a model to help you understand the relationships (cause-effect) between variables, to predict outcomes, and to help explain phenomena. (A model is an abstraction from reality. Most of the things people work with in their jobs are too big, too expensive, or too abstract to work with in real life, so they construct models. Certainly, time is an abstract concept, and we believe that the best way to work with these components is to put them into a model.)

The components of the model interrelate as follows: First, our use, or misuse, of time is largely a function of our environment, experience, and individual characteristics. Therefore, we must understand our environment, our experience, and our individual characteristics if we are going to be better users of time. The major time wasters, as listed in Figure 2-1 and 2-2, are primarily environmental or experiential or they relate to individual characteristics. Thus, a comprehensive knowledge of our environment, experience, and individual characteristics leads to the awareness component. Once we become aware, we can take action. This action leads to our ultimate goal – improved performance.

This relationship is clearer in Figure 3-7, which summarizes the relationship between the T.I.M.E. model components.

4
DIMENSIONS OF THE MODEL

11 A.M.
November 26

Now that we have explained the components of the model and their relationship, we will construct a model of time using the components that we have defined and discussed. This is one of the most important segments of the book, so we encourage you to read carefully!

The Dimensions

In order to continue with the construction of the model that began in Chapter 3, we will use the concept of ***dimensions***.

Dimension 1: Point of Reference

The first of the three dimensions that we are considering is the ***point of reference*** (see Figure 4-1). The scale indicated in Figure 4-1 represents the reference to all things from the point of view of where we are right now. As can be seen from the figure, the point of reference has the range of past, present, and future. As will be seen, some of the components can be placed in the past, some in the present, and some in the future, and some will overlap.

Dimension 2: Degree of Control

The second dimension is the ***degree of control*** (see Figure 4-2). This has a range of little to great, representing the extent to which you can in-

Figure 4-1 A Scale Representation of the Point of Reference Dimension of the Model

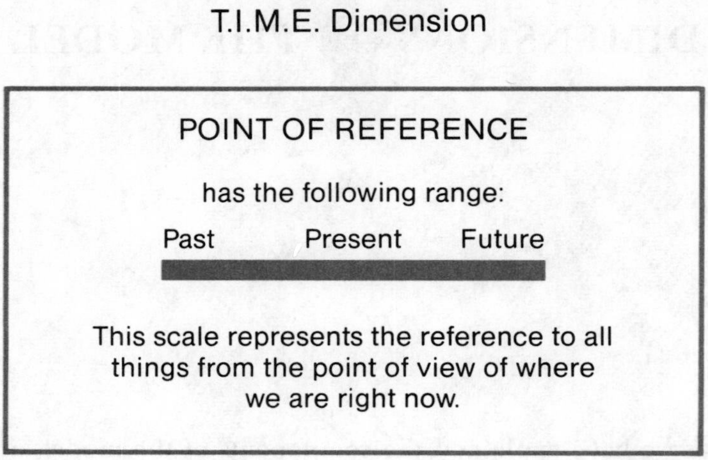

T.I.M.E. Dimension

POINT OF REFERENCE

has the following range:

Past Present Future

This scale represents the reference to all things from the point of view of where we are right now.

fluence the components of the T.I.M.E. model. You have a great deal of control over some things in your lives, and over others you have very little control.

Figure 4-2 A Scale Representation of the Degree of Control Dimension of the Model

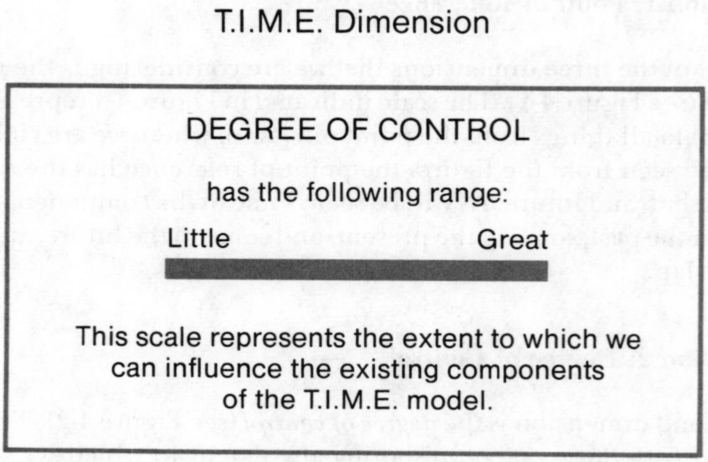

T.I.M.E. Dimension

DEGREE OF CONTROL

has the following range:

Little Great

This scale represents the extent to which we can influence the existing components of the T.I.M.E. model.

Dimension 3: Focus

Figure 4-3 represents the next dimension of interest. We have named this dimension ***focus***. This isn't a scale like the other two dimensions, but rather, it has two distinct categories — internal, or the self, and external, or the world (see Figure 4-3).

This dimension is perhaps the most difficult to understand. If you refer to the components of the model, you can see that some are part of *us as individuals* and some are *external forces.* Later we will place the components into the model, and this distinction will become clearer.

Figure 4-3 An Explanation of the Focus Dimension of the Model

T.I.M.E. Dimension

FOCUS

is dichotomous and refers to the location of the components of the T.I.M.E. model. Components of the model are part of *either* oneself or the world.

Internal — External

Unlike the other two dimensions, this one has two distinctive points — internal (self) and external (world).

Component-Dimension Relationships

Let's review the three dimensions in relation to Figure 4-4. The dimensions are arranged so that they form a box. The three dimensions represent the three dimensions of the box.

The first dimension, point of reference, represents the dimension of this figure from left to right. It divides the box into three areas, labeled *past, present,* and *future*. The second dimension, degree of control, is used

Figure 4-4 The Dimensions of the T.I.M.E. Model

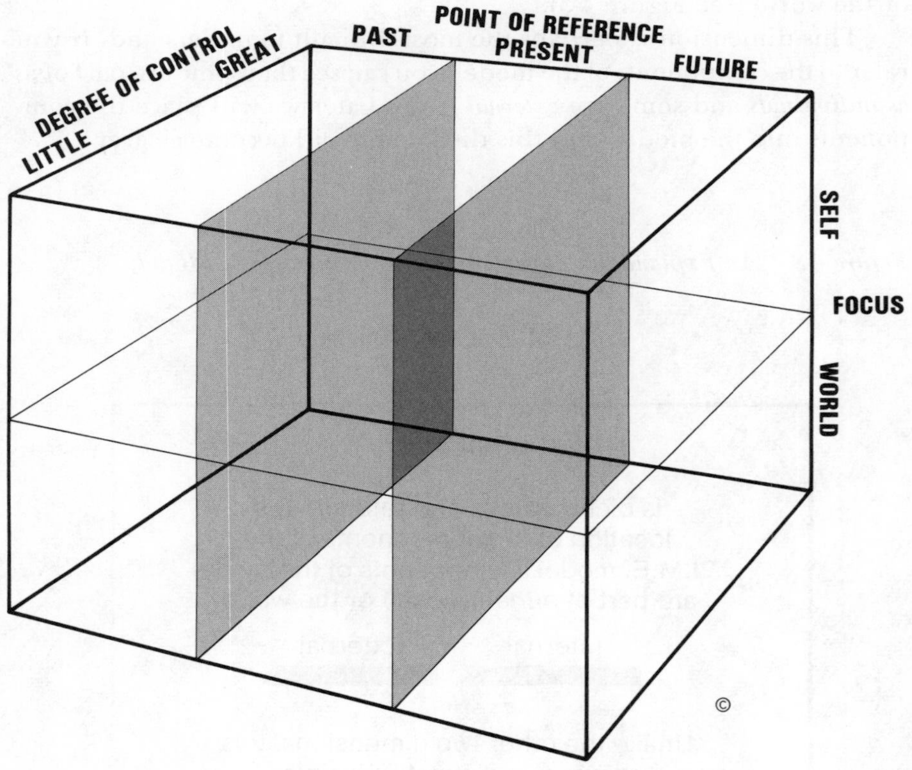

to label the dimension of the box that runs from the front to the back. This label ranges from *little* control in the front of the box to a *great deal* of control in the back. The third dimension, called focus, divides the box into top and bottom sections. The top half refers to the *self*, while the lower half refers to the *world* around you.

Now we can take the six components – environment, experience, individual characteristics, awareness, action, and improved performance – and insert them into this three-dimensional area. The important thing to note is that the six components are positioned at locations within the box based on:

1. The component's point of reference in time

2. The degree of control you have over the component
3. Whether the component focuses on you or on the world

In Figure 4-5, environment is located in the front lower left portion of the box because our environment is first of all something over which we have very little control. It represents something that is part of the world rather than part of the self and is, for the most part, in the past. Although most of our environment is recalled from our past, some of it is in the present. This is shown by a small portion of the environment block being placed in the present in Figure 4-5.

Experience is also located mainly in the past with a small portion in

Figure 4-5 The Six Components Placed in the Dimension of the T.I.M.E. Model

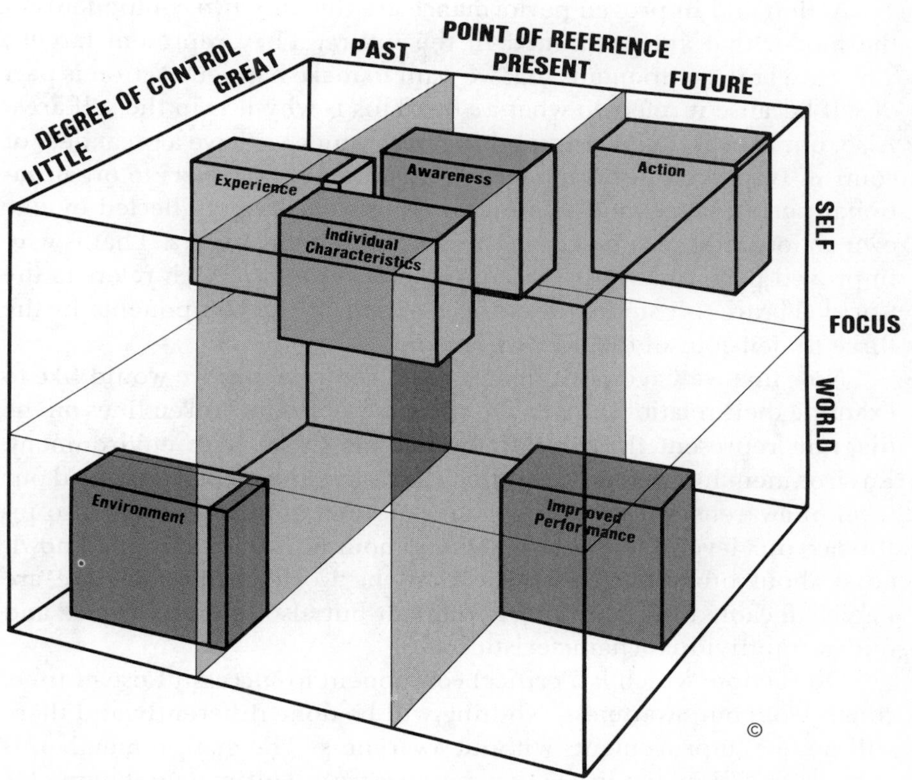

the present because although we have accrued a great deal of past experience, we rely on a small portion of that experience all the time. Notice that this component is positioned farther to the rear of the box because this component is under greater control than environment. However, it certainly is not as much under our influence as some of the other components. Experience defines part of ourselves rather than our world, so this component is positioned in the top region of the box.

The component, individual characteristics, is also considered to be a part of ourselves, but we tend to have less control over what makes up this component. That is why this component is positioned in the self area but in the forward part of the box. It is something about us that refers to the present self, since we exhibit individual characteristics at all times.

Our awareness of ourselves and of the circumstances around us is always in the present, and we have a considerable degree of control over that awareness. Awareness is a cognitive process, so it is considered part of ourselves. Based on these determinations, the component of awareness is positioned at the top center of the box, near the rear. This position reflects awareness in terms of the three dimensions.

Action and improved performance are the only two components of the model that are positioned in the future. They represent targets. They are both components that we want to make happen. Action is part of self because it refers to what *we* do. This is why it is in the self area. Also, our own actions are something over which we have a great deal of control. Improved performance, on the other hand, refers to organizational performance, and although it is to some extent affected by our own actions, it is also based on the actions of many others. That is why improved performance is placed in the lower area, which refers to the world. Figure 4-5 summarizes the location of the components in the three dimensions of the T.I.M.E. model.

Now that we have positioned the six components, we would like to examine their relationships (refer to Figure 4-6). The broken lines on the diagram represent these relationships. Let's start with environment. Environment influences individual characteristics, experience, and our level of awareness. Individual characteristics and experiences also influence our level of awareness. Much about ourselves and our knowledge about other things comes from the world around us. We are knowledgeable of not only environment but also our experience and our own individual characteristics.

Our action, which is a critical component to successful use of time, comes from our awareness. Nothing will be done differently and there will be few improvements without awareness. The goal, remember, is *appropriate* action, not just action, because we are ultimately striving for

Figure 4-6 The T.I.M.E. Model

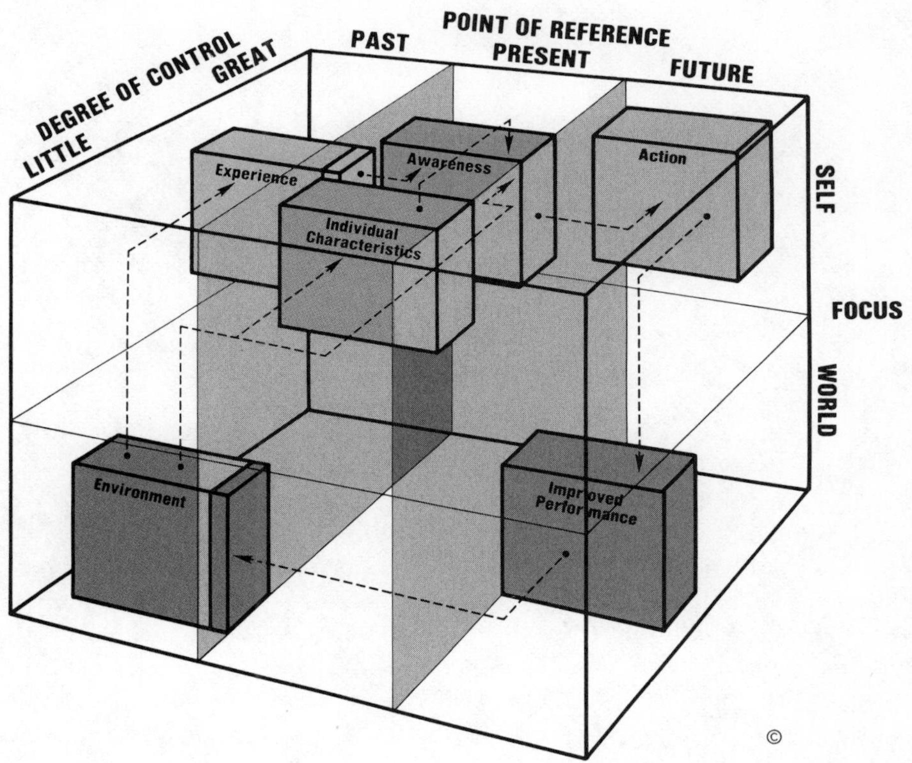

improved performance. And, to the greatest extent possible, we want to improve performance through action.

The last connection is between improved performance and environment. This is because as time passes, regardless of the level of improved performance, the results achieved become part of our environment. Together, the broken lines thus represent a continuous cycle.

5
TIME WASTERS AND THE T.I.M.E. MODEL

1 P.M.
November 26

We should now have a clear understanding of the components of the T.I.M.E. model, its dimensions, and how the components and dimensions interrelate. The objective of this chapter is to relate your time wasters to the T.I.M.E. model. This practical application will start to show you how the T.I.M.E. model can be used to improve your use of managerial time.

Recall the time wasters introduced in Chapter 2 (see Figure 2-1). You should concentrate on these primary misuses of time and relate them to the T.I.M.E. model.

Look at Figure 5-1 for a moment. This figure is a representation of the T.I.M.E. model. Note that arrows have been drawn to three of the components of the model from the left-hand margin. The purpose of these arrows is to relate time wasters to the various components of the T.I.M.E. model. Lines have been drawn next to the arrows. The number of lines provided for each component of Figure 5-1 is arbitrary. If you need more room, add lines to the appropriate component.

Before you begin this exercise, you may find it useful to review the meaning, or makeup, of these components. The primary factors that affect each of the six components are listed in Figure 5-2.

You are going to classify the major time wasters listed in Figure 2-1 by using the three components of the T.I.M.E. model listed in Figure 5-1. Not everyone will agree on how time wasters should be classified. What is important is for you to think of your business, your work, and your organization and to classify the time wasters that apply to you by using the environment, experience, and individual characteristics components of the model. Take the next ten minutes to complete this exercise.

Figure 5-1 Classifying Time Wasters by Using Three Components of the T.I.M.E. Model

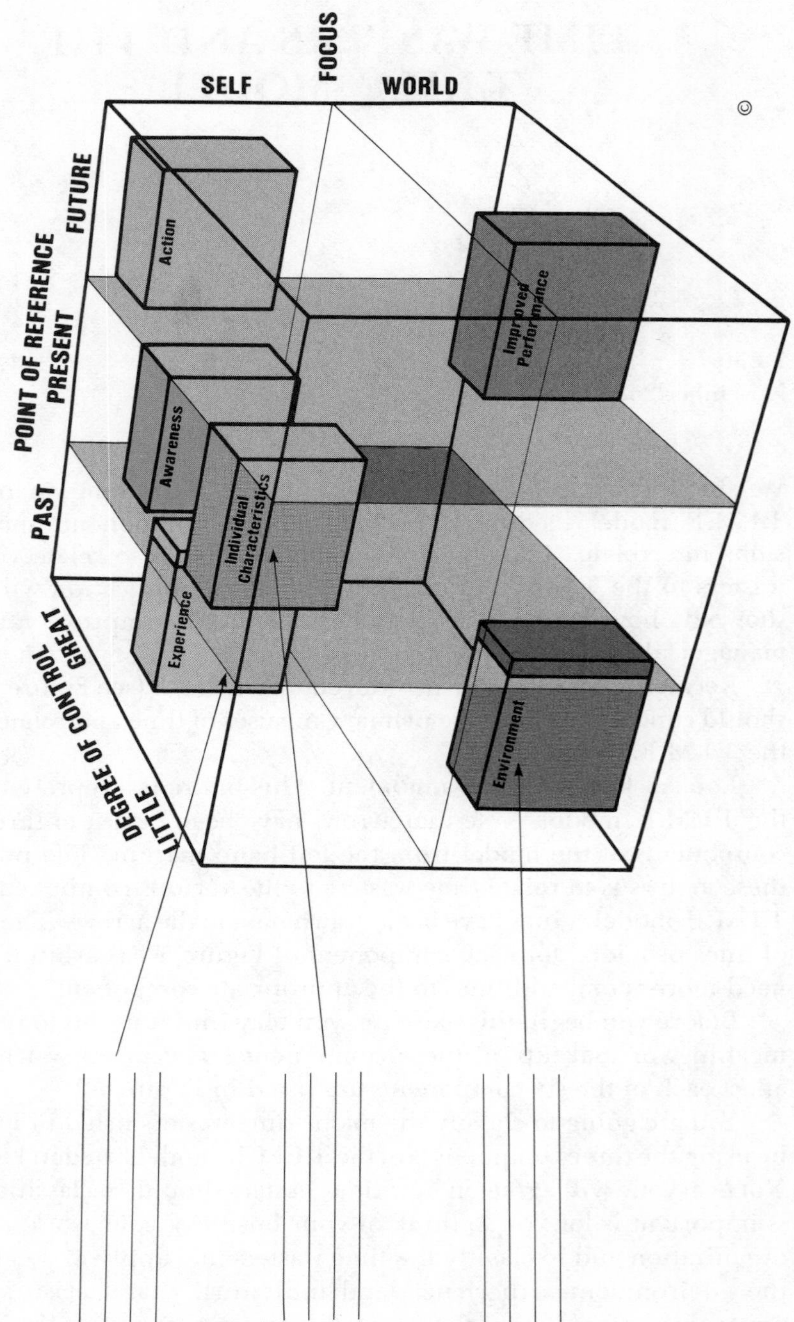

Figure 5-2 The Factors That Influence the Major Components of the T.I.M.E. Model

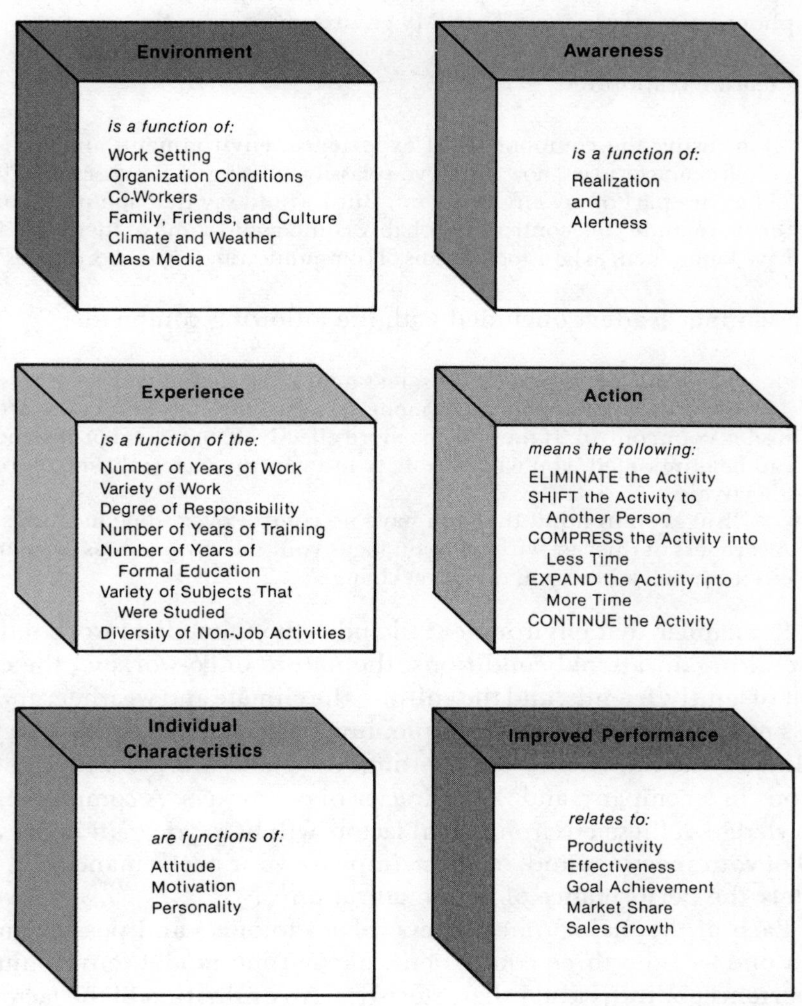
Environment
is a function of:
Work Setting
Organization Conditions
Co-Workers
Family, Friends, and Culture
Climate and Weather
Mass Media
Awareness
is a function of:
Realization
and
Alertness
Experience
is a function of the:
Number of Years of Work
Variety of Work
Degree of Responsibility
Number of Years of Training
Number of Years of
Formal Education
Variety of Subjects That
Were Studied
Diversity of Non-Job Activities
Action
means the following:
ELIMINATE the Activity
SHIFT the Activity to
Another Person
COMPRESS the Activity into
Less Time
EXPAND the Activity into
More Time
CONTINUE the Activity
Individual
Characteristics
are functions of:
Attitude
Motivation
Personality
Improved Performance
relates to:
Productivity
Effectiveness
Goal Achievement
Market Share
Sales Growth

Was your experience in classifying the wasters similar to that of Ron Holland and the other seminar participants? Observe, for a moment, their thoughts on classifying two time wasters:

> Bob Koski was called upon to comment on whether telephone interruptions are a part of his environment, experience, or individual characteristics. He hesitated for a moment, then said, "My environment."

"What do the rest of you think?" asked the seminar leader.

> Christina Jones nodded in agreement and explained: "Because of the open office environment I work in, I get interrupted constantly by the phones of workers around me. My environment is hectic."

The leader responded:

> "Ron, using the components of experience, environment, and individual characteristics, how would you classify meetings?" Ron responded: "They are part of my environment. But I would say that about half of them are under my control. I probably could avoid some of them, but I have found them to be a good means of communicating with subordinates."

The seminar leader concluded with the following comments:

> "Starting with Ron's perceptions, let's generalize a bit about meetings. They are part of your environment. Some — the ones you call — are under your control. If they can be more effectively managed or if some can be eliminated, you will be able to use your managerial time more effectively.
>
> "But keep in mind that you have no control over some meetings. Awareness of this fact will help you focus your energy on areas of your environment where you *can* effect change."

Remember that environment includes the immediate work setting; general organizational conditions; the nature of co-workers; the character of family, friends, and the culture; the climate and weather; and the mass media. Meetings, for example, involve a number of these factors, including the immediate work setting, the general organizational conditions in a company, and the character of co-workers. A comprehensive knowledge of these environmental factors will help you gain better control of your meetings and, in effect, improve your performance and ultimately the performance of the organization.

Each of the major time wasters relates to one — and possibly more than one — of the three components of the time model: environment, experience, or individual characteristics. An evaluation of the factors of that component and how the time waster relates to those factors is a beginning point for changing time wasters into time tactics. The procedure can be described as follows:

First, relate the time waster to the appropriate component of the T.I.M.E. model. Then, evaluate precisely how this waster relates to the factors that affect that component. If you waste time by procrastination and classify procrastination as an individual characteristic, you can then attack the cause of this procrastination by evaluating factors such as attitudes, motivation, and personality. Misuse of managerial time can be corrected most effectively if you relate the abuse to the factors that make up the components of the T.I.M.E. model.

In summary, you can use the T.I.M.E. model as a vehicle for improving the use of managerial time. First, delineate how you use time. Second, identify the wasters of time. Third, relate each time waster to one of the three components. Fourth, evaluate how the time wasters relate to those factors that make up the component under consideration. It may be a component that is external to you, in the past, and one over which you have little control. In these situations, you should not waste much effort attempting to correct the abuses of time. Conversely, the time waster may relate to something that pertains directly to you, is in the present, and is something over which you have a great deal of control. Thus, the T.I.M.E. model is critical in helping you assess where to spend your efforts. Finally, remember that no one will achieve a hundred percent efficiency or effectiveness.

6
A PATH TO AWARENESS: THE DAILY T.I.M.E. RECORD

2 P.M.
November 26

If you are to use the T.I.M.E. model, you must understand how you employ your time and what time wasters are relevant to you. (Remember that awareness is a critical component of the T.I.M.E. model.) One important tool to determine your use and misuse of time is the Daily T.I.M.E. Record. Take a few moments to look at Figure 6-1.

The Daily T.I.M.E. Record starts with a space for goal specification—that is, what you want to accomplish in a particular day. This part of the Daily T.I.M.E. Record has space to list activities that take place during the day. Third, you can specify the priority or importance of those activities. Fourth, you can write an assessment of those activities.

The Daily T.I.M.E. Record is most useful if information is recorded throughout the day. In other words, about every hour and a half you should write down what has occurred. The accuracy of the records will be significantly reduced if it is filled out at the day's end. At the end of the day you should set aside about half an hour to determine the importance of the day's activities and to assess these activities—that is, what went wrong and what went right. In some cases it may be beneficial to do this more than once a day. As you evaluate, you should be getting ideas about how to improve your performance. Specific time abusers and wasters should be identified. Also, at day's end you can make an assessment regarding the degree to which stated goals are achieved.

To understand more completely how to use the Daily T.I.M.E. Record and how to avoid a major pitfall, an example is useful. The events that occurred to Ron Holland on November 16, as described in Chapter 1, will be the basis for this and other examples. Figure 6-2 presents an inappropriate execution of the Daily T.I.M.E. Record. A

Figure 6-1 An Example of a Daily T.I.M.E. Record

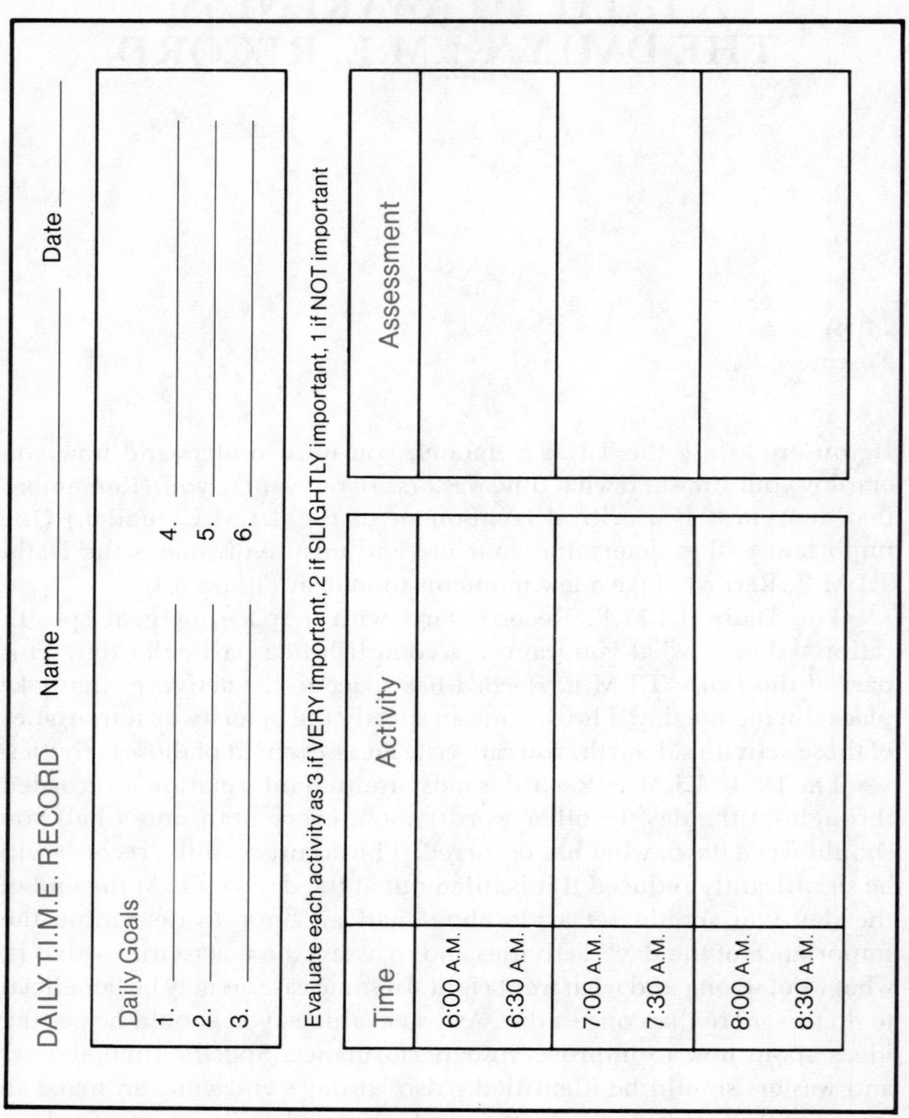

DAILY T.I.M.E. RECORD Name ______ Date ______

Daily Goals

1. ______ 4. ______
2. ______ 5. ______
3. ______ 6. ______

Evaluate each activity as 3 if VERY important, 2 if SLIGHTLY important, 1 if NOT important

Time	Activity	Assessment
6:00 A.M.		
6:30 A.M.		
7:00 A.M.		
7:30 A.M.		
8:00 A.M.		
8:30 A.M.		

Figure 6-1 (continued)

DAILY T.I.M.E. RECORD

Instructions:

1. Before you start the day, list specific goals that you would like to achieve during the day. There is space on the Daily T.I.M.E. Record for six goals.

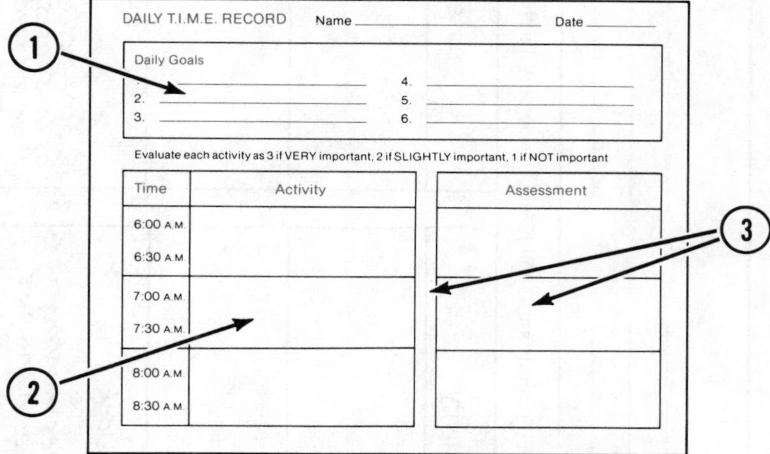

2. As you go through the day, record your activities. Your record is much more accurate if you make entries every hour rather than waiting until the end of the day.

3. After you have completed the day's activities, score each activity and write your own assessment of the day's activities. Place a 3 next to each activity that you consider to have been VERY important in completing your goals, a 2 for the SLIGHTLY important, and a 1 for those activities you felt were NOT important in achieving your goals. Use your assessments to suggest improvements.

Figure 6-2 Inappropriate Completion of the Daily T.I.M.E. Record

DAILY T.I.M.E. RECORD Name ______ Date ______

Daily Goals

1. ______ 4. ______
2. ______ 5. ______
3. ______ 6. ______

Evaluate each activity as 3 if VERY important, 2 if SLIGHTLY important, 1 if NOT important

Time	Activity		Assessment
6:00 A.M.			
6:30 A.M.			
7:00 A.M.			
7:30 A.M.			
8:00 A.M.	*Arrived at work.*		
8:30 A.M.	*Monthly sales meeting – District sales managers.*	*3*	*A good meeting – informed as to sales status in the four districts.*

Figure 6-2 (continued)

Time	Activity		Assessment
9:00 A.M.			
9:30 A.M.			
10:00 A.M.	Meeting with Gloria Alvarez.	2	Gloria seems to be a capable person. Handles delegation well.
10:30 A.M.			
11:00 A.M.			
11:30 A.M.	Left for lunch with Mrs. Komuro.	3	Great - a good new account.
12:00 P.M.			
12:30 P.M.			
1:00 P.M.	Arrived back at office.		
1:30 P.M.			

Figure 6-2 (continued)

Time	Activity		Assessment
2:00 P.M.	Worked on paperwork.	2	Get paperwork categorized.
2:30 P.M.			Good progress.
3:00 P.M.			
3:30 P.M.	End of recorded data.		
4:00 P.M.			
4:30 P.M.			
5:00 P.M.			
5:30 P.M.			
6:00 P.M.			
EVENING			

Figure 6-3 Appropriate Completion of the Daily T.I.M.E. Record

DAILY T.I.M.E. RECORD Name *Ron Holland* Date *16 Nov. 19-*

Daily Goals

1. *District Sales Managers Meeting*
2. *Meeting Gloria Alvarez - Warehouse Mgr.*
3. *Luncheon meeting Mrs. Komuro - new client*
4. *Office paperwork*
5.
6.

Evaluate each activity as 3 if VERY important, 2 if SLIGHTLY important, 1 if NOT important

Time	Activity		Assessment
6:00 A.M. 6:30 A.M.	*Up at 6:30. Assess day's activity, set daily goals.*		
7:00 A.M. 7:30 A.M.	*Left for work - 7:45*		
8:00 A.M. 8:30 A.M.	*Talked with Jim Sheard for 15 min. non-business discussion.* *NOTE: Secretary arrived at 8:16* ← *Monthly sales meeting - district sales managers.*	1 3	*Wasted 15 min. - some socializing is necessary, but it could be limited.* *Not a serious problem, but something to watch.* *Good Mtg. - I feel current regarding sales activity.*

Figure 6-3 (continued)

Time	Activity		Assessment
9:00 A.M. 9:30 A.M.	Monthly sales meeting Continued.		NOTE: Meeting went over scheduled time by ½ hour.
10:00 A.M. 10:30 A.M.	NOTE: Meeting with Gloria Alvarez: Could not find paperwork. Started work - fringe benefit pkg. Distracted - phone conversation - warehousing rack system.	2 2	Need to talk to secretary re: nec. paperwork for mtg. Should not have let phone interruption distract current activity.
11:00 A.M. 11:30 A.M.	Took another call on Jim Sheard's customer. Left for luncheon - Mrs. Komuro.	3	Should have directed it to Sheard. Need to talk to secretary.
12:00 P.M. 12:30 P.M.	Luncheon - Mrs. Komuro		Excellent meeting. Looks like good client.
1:00 P.M. 1:30 P.M.	Messages from Lute, Mead, Specker & Thomas. Called Eric Mead - talked for ½ hour.	1	Should have made it shorter. Need to get back to OSHA, Alan Specker, & Dan Thomas.

Figure 6-3 (continued)

Time	Activity	Assessment
2:00 P.M.	Reviewed report Gloria Alvarez re: fuel consumption.	1 Need to allow time for paperwork. Should give better direction regarding report.
2:30 P.M.		
3:00 P.M.		
3:30 P.M.	Finished Alvarez report.	
4:00 P.M.		
4:30 P.M.		
5:00 P.M.		
5:30 P.M.		
6:00 P.M.		
EVENING		

review of Figure 6-2 shows that only major activities are listed. In addition, specific goals for the day were not identified. Assessment is very generalized, and most of the assessment comments are not action oriented – something that would help the individual understand the type of time waster that might be involved.

Analysis of Figure 6-3 reveals quite a different picture. First, Ron has filled out his daily goals. He was aware of the fact that he had a sales managers meeting, a meeting with the warehouse manager, and lunch with a new client, and he also had some time allocated for office paperwork. Second, the activity list was structured as the day's events passed. The detailed listing of activities makes assessment easier and more useful. Figure 6-3 demonstrates that degrees of importance were assigned to specific activities at the day's end. The assessment section indicates specific problems associated with each activity.

In some instances, Table 6-3 identifies time wasters that can directly be applied to the T.I.M.E. model. The assessment comments also help Ron restructure goals for the following day. For one example, reference to one o'clock would suggest to Ron that one of his priorities for November 17 would be to contact the OSHA representative, Alan Specker, and Becky Thomas. Review of the activities for November 16, under the assessment column, would also demonstrate that Holland needs to discuss the overall work performance of his secretary. Her late arrival at the office, not having material ready for a meeting with Ms. Alvarez, and not filtering telephone calls may be areas where she needs to change her behavior. It should be noted that secretarial performance may be identified as a major time waster. This, in turn, should be related to the T.I.M.E. model – probably the experience component. Reasoning further, Ron should focus on such factors as his secretary's *training, formal education, and years of experience* to correct this abuse of time.

The Daily T.I.M.E. Record is therefore a tool for making us aware of how we use time. Once we are aware, we can act, which, in turn, will help us to improve our performance.

You may be wondering how long you should employ a Daily T.I.M.E. Record. It is a difficult question to answer; however, there are some general guidelines. If you have never used one before, it is not inappropriate to keep records for a couple of weeks. Once this amount of data is collected, you can make some assessments as to specific areas that are prominent time wasters. This can be followed by a span of time, four to six weeks, in which you can apply the time waster to the model. After about six weeks, the Daily T.I.M.E. Record can again be employed. Through a few reiterations of this process – using the Daily T.I.M.E. Record to become aware of how you use time, applying the time wasters to the model, and then evaluating the specific factors of the model – you can improve individual and organizational performance.

You should be able to correct the most flagrant time wasters in approximately one to one and a half years. After that period, you can start to pay attention to the more subtle issues of time use. This involves the same process we have discussed, but it deals with more sophisticated aspects of managerial time. The appendix includes some blank forms of the Daily T.I.M.E. Record for your use.

7
A PATH TO ACTION: T.I.M.E. TACTICS

3 P.M.
November 26

We have introduced the T.I.M.E. model and have identified the classic time wasters and related them to three of the model's components (environment, experience, and individual characteristics). We have reviewed the relevance and use of the Daily T.I.M.E. Record as a means of becoming aware of how managers use time. It is now appropriate to move from awareness to action. Action, as we previously stated, is executing the appropriate strategy. Action suggests positive moves to correct deficiencies or to solve problems. What we will be doing, then, is transforming time wasters into T.I.M.E. Tactics. T.I.M.E. Tactics are *positive* interpretations of time wasters. The telephone, for example, can be a time saver if it is used correctly. Each time waster must be translated into a positive, rather than a negative, action.

In Figure 7-1, you can see how the major time wasters have been transformed into T.I.M.E. Tactics. You can also begin to see that what we are suggesting is really very dramatic—that the time wasters, when appropriately managed, become time tactics. We will now relate each T.I.M.E. Tactic to other concepts we have presented.

The T.I.M.E. Tactics

T.I.M.E. Tactic 1: Use the Telephone Wisely

The action required to turn the first time waster—telephone interruptions—into a T.I.M.E. Tactic is a change from habitual, casual behavior to thoughtful action. The first item in Figure 7-2 suggests that a prelimi-

Figure 7-1 T.I.M.E. Tactics Matched with Time Wasters

T.I.M.E. Tactics

MAJOR TIME WASTERS	T.I.M.E. TACTICS
1. Telephone interruptions.	1. Use the telephone wisely.
2. Drop-in visitors.	2. Control visitors.
3. Misused meetings.	3. Manage meetings.
4. Crisis management.	4. Expect the unexpected.
5. Lack of objectives, priorities, daily plan.	5. Set objectives and priorities.
6. Cluttered desk / personal disorganization.	6. Get your world organized.
7. Ineffective delegation of responsibilities.	7. Delegate effectively.
8. Attempting too much at once.	8. Budget activities.
9. Insufficient and unclear communications.	9. Communicate effectively.
10. Indecision.	10. Make decisions.
11. Procrastination.	11. Get motivated.
12. Inability to say no.	12. Say no.
13. Leaving tasks unfinished.	13. Finish tasks.
14. Lack of self-discipline.	14. Develop self-discipline.

Figure 7-2 T.I.M.E. Tactic 1: Use the Telephone Wisely

T.I.M.E. Tactic

USE THE TELEPHONE WISELY

1. Use the Daily T.I.M.E. Record to log telephone calls, and periodically analyze your log.
2. Avoid a lot of personal calls.
3. Allocate a time for making phone calls.
4. Plan what you are going to say before calling.
5. If possible, have someone screen your calls.
6. Develop the confidence to keep conversations short.
7. Keep a directory of frequently called numbers.
8. Utilize the newest telephone equipment and service.

nary move to this action is using the Daily T.I.M.E. Record to analyze how you use the phone.

Prioritizing return calls is an important principle to apply to telephone use. Some return calls are more important than others, and responses to such calls must be quicker. In many instances, subordinates or secretaries may be able to return calls. Categorizing calls based on importance can help the manager realize the various options for responding.

Wise use of the phone also suggests a minimum of personal calls. Do you exchange several calls with family members several times a day? If so, you will probably want to review the need for those calls. If some are unnecessary and can be eliminated, you will save time. Another way to use the telephone wisely is to make group calls. Planning what you want to say helps make calls shorter and prevents further calls. If you have a secretary, you might want to have him or her screen calls. But what if you don't have a secretary?

Let's take the example of Christina Jones, the office manager for Security Mutual Insurance. We will use the T.I.M.E. model and see what action is appropriate. If we argue that the telephone is part of her environment, then we must analyze the phone in that context. If Ms. Jones can't gain support to have someone do the screening because of the nature of her immediate work setting, she will have to limit her action to other tactics. She can, for example, avoid many personal calls, make outgoing calls at specified times, plan what she needs to say in those calls, keep the calls short and to the topic at hand, develop a directory of frequently called numbers, and investigate relevant new telephone technology. For instance, she might research the idea of using a telephone recorder. Analysis may determine that it is not feasible, but it is worth investigation. In other words, Ms. Jones may not be able to have her calls screened, but she can try the seven other action items suggested in Figure 7-2. You must consider a T.I.M.E. Tactic in the context of your own job using the relevant component of the T.I.M.E. model.

T.I.M.E. Tactic 2: Control Visitors

A second T.I.M.E. Tactic is to control visitors. Figure 7-3 describes some basic actions that are appropriate for this T.I.M.E. Tactic. Here again the Daily T.I.M.E. Record can be helpful. Also, the screening question again becomes relevant. It is critical to use your office primarily for business. Obviously some casual conversation will always occur; how-

Figure 7-3 T.I.M.E. Tactic 2: Control Visitors

T.I.M.E. Tactic

CONTROL VISITORS

1. Use the Daily T.I.M.E. Record to log the time spent visiting.
2. If possible, have someone screen your visitors.
3. Use your office for business activities and let others know this.
4. Do not overdo the open-door policy. Make sure you have time to yourself.

ever, the critical point is to control it. An open-door policy can help you accomplish certain managerial tasks, but don't overdo that policy and waste time.

Most artists, musicians, and scientists find that there's a time when they are at their most creative and effective – when they can give full attention to their tasks and objectives. Managers should also discover their periods of peak efficiency. Such blocks of time should be carefully protected from visitors and other interruptions. Staff personnel should be advised to interrupt only for emergencies or very important problems. Less important problems should be postponed until the manager's period of concentration is over.

T.I.M.E. Tactic 3: Manage Meetings

The third tactic is the management of meetings. Take a look at Figure 7-4.

Figure 7-4 T.I.M.E. Tactic 3: Manage Meetings

T.I.M.E. Tactic

MANAGE MEETINGS

1. Make sure each meeting has a purpose.
2. Use an agenda.
3. Distribute the agenda before the meeting.
4. Invite only those who are needed.
5. Select the location and identify a time period consistent with the meeting's purpose.
6. Evaluate the need for any meeting.
7. Start and end meetings on time.
8. Take minutes.
9. Summarize activities and review assignments.

Chairperson

The problem some managers have is they cannot find a good chairperson and thus end up running the meeting themselves. If this happens to you, try choosing some of your best subordinates and training them to manage meetings. Delegate this task formally and appraise their performance in accomplishing the objectives immediately after the meeting.

Whether you are the chairperson or just a participant, you can take several steps to improve the effectiveness of a meeting. When a meeting is called, find out what it is about; identify its objectives. Another important action is to identify other employees who will be attending. This information will help to clarify the roles of others and your role and what might be expected of you. Read reports, memos, and other source documents to prepare for the meeting.

The role of the chairperson is to guide the meeting in several ways. First, the chair makes sure that the meeting starts and ends on time. Second, the chair ensures that participants are prepared. Advance distribution of an agenda helps to accomplish this goal. Last, the chairperson should summarize conclusions and reach an agreement on the necessity for future meetings.

T.I.M.E. Tactic 4: Expect the Unexpected

Another important point is that most tasks take longer to complete than you think. Thus, always expect the unexpected (see Figure 7-5). It does not pay to be caught off guard. We allocate time to achieve daily goals,

Figure 7-5 T.I.M.E. Tactic 4: Expect the Unexpected

T.I.M.E. Tactic

EXPECT THE UNEXPECTED

1. Record and analyze unexpected events.
2. Identify the causes of unexpected events.
3. Leave time for the unexpected.
4. Remember, tasks generally take longer than you think.

and we should also allocate time for unexpected problems and opportunities that may arise. These new opportunities may become tomorrow's goals. Thus, our plans should contain flexibility for better opportunities as well as for responses to unforeseen problems.

Keeping a record of crises that interrupt goal achievement can help to assess their probability of occurrence. You may find that there is actually a pattern to their activity. Developing a plan to handle these situations can also help. For example, situations can be classified as "crisis interruptions," which have to be dealt with immediately, or as "general interruptions," which can be predicted and maybe avoided.

T.I.M.E. Tactic 5: Set Objectives and Priorities

When you are setting objectives, remember that objectives must be attainable, measurable, acceptable to employees, affordable, and congruent with other job tasks (see Figure 7-6). The Daily T.I.M.E. Record can help you identify objectives. The next step is to establish priorities among the daily objectives, then to set deadlines for their achievement. With this type of planning, your results will be more predictable than if you trust to chance.

How do you get subordinates to commit themselves to objectives? You might try basing rewards and performance evaluations directly on

Figure 7-6 T.I.M.E. Tactic 5: Set Objectives and Priorities

T.I.M.E. Tactic

SET OBJECTIVES AND PRIORITIES

1. Use a Daily T.I.M.E. Record.
2. Use deadlines for important objectives.
3. Describe your objectives so that you can clearly identify when they have been completed.
4. Remember that your best chance of success comes from the knowledge of what has to be done.

the subordinates' achievement of objectives. People have to realize that objective achievement is an important part of their job. Another possible action is to ask subordinates to develop their own objectives. This will engage them in the process and help them form the habit of setting objectives. When you do this, be sure to keep your subordinates informed of your own objectives and the organizational goals.

Tying objectives together can help managers and subordinates to visualize how one goal acts as a component in a chain of goals that ultimately links up to company-wide goals. Recognizing their participation in achieving corporate goals can spur employees to increase their commitment and the energy they expend toward achieving their objectives.

Objectives imply commitment. Attention must be directed toward objectives and effort directed into activities that will lead to achievement of objectives. Deadlines should be established so that progress toward achievement of an objective can be assessed; progress should be periodically reviewed. New objectives should be developed on the basis of progress made toward achievement of previous objectives.

T.I.M.E. Tactic 6: Get Your World Organized

You cannot effectively set and achieve objectives without organizing

Figure 7-7 T.I.M.E. Tactic 6: Get Your World Organized

T.I.M.E. Tactic

GET YOUR WORLD ORGANIZED

1. Organize your world.
2. Tackle the highest priority item first.
3. Set aside time during the day for *your* work.
4. Organize the information that you receive.
5. Get help if you need it.

your environment. Let's focus for a moment on how to do this by looking at Figure 7-7. Note that the first suggestion, organize your world, is almost the same as the T.I.M.E. Tactic. The suggestion, though, is meant to be very specific. For example, it is difficult to work on a cluttered desk. Items can become lost, and you can be distracted too easily. Whenever you begin to work on one project, something else catches your eye and captures your thoughts. You may have wasted considerable time before you return to the work at hand. Therefore, the first action to take is to put in order your current projects, background information, and tools.

Another way to organize your world is to make sure that you set priorities and then tackle the top priority items first. For example, achieving five other objectives but failing to complete a crucial report in time for a meeting could be disastrous. Always keep in mind your objectives and priorities and spend your time where it will be most effective.

If two or more objectives have the same priority, a good rule is to tackle the toughest task first. This calls for ranking jobs from the easiest to the most difficult. As your work time passes, a feeling of accomplishment will emerge as a result of achieving difficult tasks, and lesser energy can be devoted to simpler tasks. Also remember that most people are more alert in the morning than in the afternoon hours. Thus, it is generally wise to start the most difficult tasks in the morning.

Good filing systems are a necessity for today's busy manager. The ability to store and retrieve information efficiently is a critical time saver. Even if you have a secretary to do this for you, time is wasted when important documents and reports cannot be located quickly. In today's business environment, every manager should at least consider the use of a computer to store and retrieve much of the necessary data. This is more efficient and is certainly quicker. Remember, too, that not everything needs to be filed. The more unnecessary filing that takes place, the more time is wasted, both in the filing process itself and in the increased difficulty in locating what is needed. Also, periodically evaluate your file system for efficiency, and clean out your files.

Remember to set aside time for your own work. But also remember to consider if any of your tasks can be delegated. The more you delegate, the more work will get done.

T.I.M.E. Tactic 7: Delegate Effectively

One common problem of executives is the inability to delegate work properly to subordinates. For example, some managers delegate small, unimportant tasks but fail to delegate difficult or meaningful work. Yet effective delegation is one of the best time savers. After all, you can't do it all yourself—you don't have enough time and you probably don't know enough. Also, your subordinates will never effectively do their jobs or develop their potential if you don't let them have some authority and responsibility. The more you delegate, the more effective your subordinates will become, and you can delegate still more. Many people do not delegate because they don't like to take the responsibility for someone else's work, but this is part of being a good manager. Figure 7-8 indicates some tactics that might help you to delegate more effectively.

Figure 7-8 T.I.M.E. Tactic 7: Delegate Effectively

T.I.M.E. Tactic

DELEGATE EFFECTIVELY

1. Define clearly subordinate duties and responsibilities.
2. Keep your goals and objectives in mind.
3. Help your subordinates set goals for themselves.
4. Give subordinates the authority and the resources to achieve their goals.
5. Provide rewards for work well done.
6. Be sure you know your own duties and responsibilities.
7. Develop an organization chart.

The first idea is probably the most important for the majority of us. In your own mind, decide what you should do, and then decide what your subordinates should do. Then stick to your decision except in emergencies. You may ask, "How do I decide what I should do and what others should do?" We can't tell you precisely, but you know certain things in your business are more important than others—tasks that involve more money or bigger sales, for example. One point must be made: Be realistic in your determination of what you must do. Don't keep all the easy jobs for yourself and assign all of the hard ones to your subordinates or vice versa.

It is easy to rationalize. Take, for example, a supervisor who insisted on passing out the paychecks to his subordinates each payday instead of letting his secretary do it. He claimed that he wanted to keep control of the checks to make sure they got to the right people. During a talk with him, however, he admitted that he liked to be able to walk around, joke with his subordinates about their pay, and see how they were doing. This isn't necessarily bad, but he should have asked himself if there was something more important he should be doing. Maybe he should distribute the checks once in a while, but probably not all the time. Also, he was giving his secretary the impression that he didn't trust her with the checks, which she resented.

Think about the activities you perform, and ask yourself which ones your subordinates could do just as well as, or perhaps better than, you. Delegating appropriate tasks would allow you to do what is most effective for your position. Incidentally, a review of your Daily T.I.M.E. Record will be extremely valuable in helping you determine what to delegate.

> Ron's mind wandered back to November 16, and he thought to himself, Did I really need to meet with Komuro myself on that account? It's pretty important, but maybe someone else could have handled it. I'll have to think about that.

What can you do when no one but you can handle a task? There is a simple answer to that question — an answer that is much simpler to say than to do. Decide what your subordinates should be doing, and if they can't do it, train them so they can or replace them. That's part of your job as a manager.

The fourth item in Figure 7-8 is important. If you are going to delegate, make sure that the subordinates have enough resources to effectively do what you have assigned to them. This is common sense, but we managers often forget it.

Finally, note item 5 in Figure 7-8. If you delegate to others in the organization, you must also reward them for carrying out the task. These rewards can take many forms. It is not the intent of this chapter to analyze the various types of rewards available. It is enough to say that the situation and the persons must be evaluated and that the reward chosen should be appropriate.

T.I.M.E. Tactic 8: Budget Enough Time for Activities

Another valuable time tactic is budgeting enough time for activities (see Figure 7-9). We often attempt to do too much in too little time. Remember that the word *realistic* was used in the discussion of delegating. It

Figure 7-9 T.I.M.E. Tactic 8: Budget Activities

T.I.M.E. Tactic

BUDGET ACTIVITIES

1. Decide on a realistic number of important activities to be completed.
2. Remember that jobs usually take longer than you think.
3. Make sure you clearly understand the difference between *urgent* and *important* activities.

shows up again here. You have to learn to be realistic in determining what you do during one day or one week. Too often we overestimate our own ability, and this catches up with us. Also, remember that projects usually take longer than you expect. This is another good time to look at your Daily T.I.M.E. Record. If you keep this record properly, it can tell you how long it really took you to complete a task. You may be surprised.

An important key to making this tactic work for you is learning to differentiate between the words *urgent* and *important*. There's an old saying that the urgent gets done now, the important we finish at midnight. Even with good time management, you may sometimes have to work late, but with practice it happens less often. Not everything is urgent and not everything is even important. You have to use judgment.

The manager and the subordinate often have different ideas on this subject. What your manager thinks is urgent might not seem so to you, and the other way around. The best idea is to clarify the issue with your boss (or your subordinates) by asking and answering questions. It is important to be flexible, though. One of you is wrong, and it might be you.

Remember, too, that most jobs will take longer than you think they will, even if you have experience with them. There are always interruptions, and even tasks that you have performed before may have differences. A general rule is to add 10 percent to each time estimate that you make — that cushion will help you to predict more accurately. Of course, if this is the first time you are performing the task, a 10 percent cushion is probably not enough. You must use your own judgment. The important point is that we tend to underestimate the time required and overestimate our own abilities, so we need to compensate.

T.I.M.E. Tactic 9: Communicate Effectively

Most managers recognize the importance of communication in their jobs, but we often do not think of communication when we talk about effective time use. However, it certainly can be a factor. If we don't communicate effectively with our subordinates or with each other, we

Figure 7-10 *T.I.M.E. Tactic 9: Communicate Effectively*

T.I.M.E. Tactic

COMMUNICATE EFFECTIVELY

1. Identify the sender and receiver.
2. Develop objectives for the communication.
3. Develop and communicate deadlines for anticipating responses.
4. Communicate the message effectively in several ways.
5. Anticipate the main ideas of the sender and receiver.
6. Make mental and written summaries of information sent.
7. Recognize that words have different meanings.
8. Train your mind to think while communicating.

cannot expect to get the desired results. It isn't possible to devote enough time in this book, or perhaps in any book, to cover all of the topics relevant to communication, but let's take a look at some points (see Figure 7-10).

The first point, identification of the sender and the receiver, sounds very elementary — you know that you are the sender, and you know who you are sending to. But you also have to consider the ultimate receiver. You may direct a communication to the plant manager, but the persons ultimately affected may be the workers on an assembly line. You must realize this and word your communication accordingly.

Also, what is the communication supposed to do? Is it supposed to convey information or is it supposed to give directions? The objectives of the communication must be determined if it is to be effective.

> Ron concentrated on the third point, develop deadlines for anticipating responses. He thought: Boy, how many times have I given assignments to people with no deadlines, then become irritated when it wasn't on my desk when I thought it should be. I know better, but I don't always think.

This third point means more than just developing deadlines for yourself — you also have to communicate these deadlines to the people who are supposed to respond to you. Everyone gets frustrated when this isn't done. You get frustrated waiting for responses, and the people who are responding become frustrated because they don't know what their timetable is.

You might wonder why subordinates don't ask if they don't know what the deadline is. You would ask if you were in that position. But maybe they don't feel as secure as you do. Maybe they think they should know and don't want to appear dumb. Whatever the reason, you are the manager, and it is your responsibility to determine ahead of time what they need and want to know, and to tell them as much as you can. Without well-considered and well-communicated deadlines, time is wasted by all parties involved.

Notice, too, the seventh item in Figure 7-10. Words have different meanings to people based on people's background, interests, and experiences. You have to recognize this. If you communicate to your subordinates in words they misunderstand, you may get strange results. Remember, the purpose of communicating in an organization is to initiate some kind of desired action. If the receiver misinterprets words in the communication, the results may waste everyone's time or possibly even be damaging to the organization.

It is important to remember that communication is difficult. We tend to assume that everyone shares our background and objectives. How can we do a better job? This is another answer that is easy to give but hard to implement. You have to put yourself in the place of the people with whom you are communicating and use language that you think they will understand. If you are an engineer, for example, and you are talking to people who are not engineers, you can't use engineering language even though it is natural and easier for you. Remember, understanding is the goal, and most of the responsibility for achieving this understanding falls on the person communicating. If you can say something once, be understood, and reach your goals, imagine how much time you can save.

T.I.M.E. Tactic 10: Make Decisions

An example is probably the most effective way to communicate the essence of this T.I.M.E. Tactic. A speaker at a meeting began his presentation on the subject of the importance of making decisions by placing a transparency on the overhead projector. Then he placed the transparency back in his briefcase and announced, "I think it's time for a coffee break." The speaker was about halfway to the coffee pot when he stopped and looked at his watch. "No," he said, "it's getting too late. We'd better continue with the meeting." There was a dissatisfied murmur in the room as people sat down again. The speaker returned to the podium and shuffled through a series of papers. The audience grew uncomfortable, and low conversations began breaking out around the room. Then the speaker said, "I guess we should continue." He placed a transparency on the projector that said: Make Decisions. A number of people in the audience laughed as it became obvious that the speaker's actions had been intentional.

To be indecisive about what we want to do wastes time – in the example just presented, maybe five minutes. Five minutes may not be a great deal of time, but it was not a major decision either. If this had been a major decision and if the manager had been indecisive, much more time would have been wasted.

Notice what else happened in the example. The audience was disappointed when they did not do what the speaker said they were going to do – in that instance, get coffee. Some people became frustrated as the speaker was trying to make a decision. In fact, some people probably wondered about the competence of the speaker because of his inability to make a decision.

In any organization, much more than five minutes is wasted by indecision. Indecisiveness is a problem not only in major decisions but also in the small decisions that face managers dozens of times a day. If you look back at the T.I.M.E. Tactics already discussed, you will find many

Figure 7-11 T.I.M.E. Tactic 10: Make Decisions

T.I.M.E. Tactic

MAKE DECISIONS

1. Use time wisely to assemble facts.
2. Clarify goals to be achieved.
3. Take time out to assess your attitudes about goals and facts.
4. Consider alternatives that have potential.
5. Examine different conditions that exist in your environment.
6. Analyze each alternative in light of each condition.
7. Choose a workable solution and implement it.

examples: what jobs have high priority, what constitutes an emergency, what tasks could be delegated to subordinates, and so on. In fact, this system for learning to use time more effectively involves a whole series of decisions. If you never make these decisions, you can't possibly improve your time usage. Decision making is the first step.

How can you improve your decision-making ability? There are many ways that this process can be facilitated, including books on decision making, but a good start would be to study the seven steps listed in Figure 7-11. Remember that it is important to use your judgment even about following these steps. For example, don't waste time collecting unnecessary information, and eliminate unfeasible alternatives early in the decision-making process.

T.I.M.E. Tactic 11: Get Motivated

The last four tactics are not at the end because they are less important than the previous tactics. On the contrary; they can help make the difference in whether you do or do not accomplish your goals for the day.

The eleventh tactic, described in Figure 7-12, is Get Motivated. Getting motivated describes a kind of mental disposition. It means that instead of putting off things that need to be accomplished, you decide what are the long- and short-range goals and then go after them. Listing your daily goals in the Daily T.I.M.E. Record keeps them in front of you.

Figure 7-12 T.I.M.E. Tactic 11: Get Motivated

T.I.M.E. Tactic

GET MOTIVATED

1. Set both short- and long-range goals.
2. Record short-range goals into your Daily T.I.M.E. Record.
3. Rate your degree of progress toward goal achievement.
4. Work with factors inhibiting your effectiveness.
5. Redefine goals as conditions change.
6. Reassess periodically both those goals that have been achieved and those that must be achieved.

Maintaining your motivation and that of your subordinates requires that you assess the degree of progress toward goal achievement. Many times goals are not completely attained within a short period such as a day, week, or month. Assessing progress helps keep the goal in mind, acknowledges work that has been done, and places both goal and progress in perspective. Another reason for measuring progress is that the importance of goals changes. A goal partially accomplished may now be less important and should be reduced in priority in the Daily T.I.M.E. Record. Assessing your progress also alerts you if things are not proceeding as planned. You can then decide if you need to change your plans to speed things up.

When goals are not achieved, it is critical to determine the factors that have inhibited attainment. Be specific when you identify the inhibiting factors. For example, is it a lack of employee effectiveness or motivation or a lack of resources? Identifying the problem areas will lead to solutions and increase one's overall motivation.

As has been emphasized before, it is important to redefine goals as conditions change. This is especially true when crises erupt.

Learning this process will require special thought and attention, but persist. Remember that the process of getting motivated and evaluating the degree of success of goal accomplishment is an important part of an active approach to managing one's time. After a while, if you find rewards in your accomplishments, you will find the process becoming a natural part of your thinking during the day. It is almost like taking a Zen approach to the day's activities. The Zen way of doing things is to do them.

T.I.M.E. Tactic 12: Say No

The twelfth tactic, illustrated in Figure 7-13 is Say No. This task sounds simple, but its importance cannot be emphasized enough. If you are not vigilant, your day can become crammed with little (and big) activities that you should not be doing. These activities are unproductive, time consuming, and a major distraction from the activities you want and need to carry out. When these "requests" come, the answer is to say no. There are plenty of things that you must do because they are mandated by others – these alone will take care of a big part of each day. All the more reason to stop the flood of other demands when you can respond by saying no.

Before you take on additional work assignments, remember to allow time to evaluate those assignments. Are they peripheral or will they make a major contribution? Can you afford a major additional task in light of your other responsibilities? One technique that can be useful in helping you evaluate these additional assignments is to use your Daily T.I.M.E. Record. The Daily T.I.M.E. Record lists priority objectives and also contains feedback. For example, the assessment section can help you evaluate whether it is realistic for you to take on additional assignments. For the aggressive manager, it is important to recognize that there is a limit to what an individual can do. It is critical to place additional assignments in the perspective of your overall goals and your immediate work responsibilities. It is important to remember that it is not necessarily bad to say no. You can do it politely, and you can give objective reasons. Remember that if you take on too much work, you will

Figure 7-13 T.I.M.E. Tactic 12: Say No

T.I.M.E. Tactic

SAY NO

1. Allow time to evaluate an additional work assignment before accepting it.
2. Use your Daily T.I.M.E. Record to evaluate the practicality of taking on additional assignments.
3. Recognize that there is a finite limit to what you can do.
4. Consider alternative ways to say no.
5. Don't confuse more work with better work.
6. Accomplish a limited set of tasks efficiently and effectively versus a greater number of tasks poorly.

not do an effective job in accomplishing your assigned tasks. You must not confuse the concept of more work with better work.

The ability to say no requires judgment. Sometimes your work responsibilities and level of authority will require the addition of activities. However, the ability to say no can place the organization into a more healthy perspective.

T.I.M.E. Tactic 13: Finish Tasks

The thirteenth tactic, Finish Tasks (see Figure 7-14), is included to remind you that activities left unfinished have a greater chance of never being completed. When we allocate time, we can easily underestimate the time necessary to complete a task. As a result, instead of finishing something, we are forced to move on to another job, leaving the task unfinished. The time already invested in an unfinished task is wasted if the task is not finished. First be sure that a task is worth starting, then make a strong commitment to complete tasks you have begun. Use the

Daily T.I.M.E. Record to help. Using your past experience, try to make more accurate time estimates so that you plan enough time to complete the activity. If a project is new, pad the estimate in case you encounter problems. Remember the discussion of T.I.M.E. Tactic 8. When an activity is completed, use your accomplishment as a mental reward so that you are motivated to move on to the next activity on your list.

Figure 7-14 T.I.M.E. Tactic 13: Finish Tasks

T.I.M.E. Tactic

FINISH TASKS

1. Set objectives and priorities.
2. Develop a checklist; cross off items when completed.
3. Review your Daily T.I.M.E. Record to determine the importance of tasks.
4. Learn ways to allocate enough time to finish a task.
5. Use the help of others to block out adequate time for a given task.

An example will help stress the importance of finishing tasks. The morning before a 1 P.M. seminar for fifty executives, we were reviewing materials. A clerk had been assigned the responsibility of collating a rather large, complex set of handouts. We found, to our dismay, that the handouts were not collated in the right order. Fortunately, there was enough time to correct the error. When we later followed up on the problem, we discovered that the clerk had been interrupted with another assigned task. The interruption caused a two-day gap in the collation process, leading to errors about what had been collated.

To summarize, leaving tasks unfinished can lead to errors or can result in the job never being completed. It is therefore important to finish tasks, which requires the allocation of adequate time.

T.I.M.E. Tactic 14: Develop Self-Discipline

The last T.I.M.E. Tactic, Develop Self-Discipline (see Figure 7-15), is the foundation for the other thirteen tactics. You will never master the remaining tactics without developing self-discipline. Developing self-discipline and self-control is the only alternative to either no control or control by others.

Figure 7-15 T.I.M.E. Tactic 14: Develop Self-Discipline

T.I.M.E. Tactic

DEVELOP SELF-DISCIPLINE

1. Evaluate your attitude toward work.
2. Learn that planning develops and encourages self-discipline.
3. Place realistic deadlines on the accomplishment of tasks.
4. Concentrate on a task until it is completed.

One way to begin developing self-discipline is to analyze your attitude toward your work and toward your job as a whole. Are you committed to your organization, to being as effective as possible in your position, to developing your own potential and helping your subordinates and co-workers develop theirs?

Planning activities and setting realistic deadlines are ways to encourage self-discipline, but in the end, self-discipline really just means sticking to it – you must persist until the task is complete. You must also remember that self-discipline is not developed once and then forgotten; you must exercise your self-discipline to keep it healthy and strong.

A final point to remember: You can't make major changes in your life or work habits without first exercising self-discipline in what might seem like trivial matters. As the Chinese proverb teaches: "Small ills are the foundations of most of our groans. Men trip not on mountains but stumble on stones."

We have seen how fourteen common time wasters can be transformed into tactics to help you use time more effectively. You may identify a time waster that is not in this group or that is a variation or a combination of the ones listed. To deal with this time waster, carry through the logic of the T.I.M.E. model—that is, reason back to the T.I.M.E. model and evaluate the component's factors; look at the specific issues within each component; translate the time waster into positive terms, creating a T.I.M.E. Tactic; and implement the time tactic, thus taking action to improve performance. The fourteen T.I.M.E. Tactics thus function as a general guide to action.

The essence of this book is to employ the T.I.M.E. model to improve management effectiveness. In terms of the model itself, the objective is to improve performance. Ultimately, we want to be better managers, and by being better managers, help our organizations meet their goals. Along the way, we want to increase our job satisfaction and financial rewards.

The concluding chapters of the book focus on these issues—improved performance and the execution of the T.I.M.E. model—in a holistic context.

8
A PATH TO IMPROVED PERFORMANCE: T.I.M.E.

4 P.M.
November 26

It is nearly 4 P.M. and the seminar is nearing its close. The better part of the time has been spent discussing ways to improve management of time. Remember, though, that the ultimate goal is to improve management effectiveness – that is, to improve performance. As you recall, there is no one way to measure improved performance. It must be broken down to the individual level – to each job within the organization. Bob Koski thought:

> Improved performance from my perspective as controller of a corporation might be improved liquidity, profitability, and solvency. Or it might be better employee relations, which should lead to a smoother running organization and then to goals such as growth and profitability.

It is important to look at the title of this chapter: A Path to Improved Performance: T.I.M.E. The critical idea we want you to remember is that you must practice the T.I.M.E. model to achieve improved performance and become a better manager.

To see how well you understand the T.I.M.E. model, try to answer the following questions. (If you need a review, Figure 8-1 diagrams the basic ideas of the model.) First, where would you start in the overall process of employing the T.I.M.E. model? Think a few minutes, and then see how your answer compares to the answer given by Ron Holland:

> "It seems to me that the first thing one has to do is to get a clear understanding of the six components of the T.I.M.E. model. In other words, we have to describe our environment, our individual characteristics, and our experience by looking at the specific factors that make up

Figure 8-1 Conceptual Flow of the T.I.M.E. Model Process

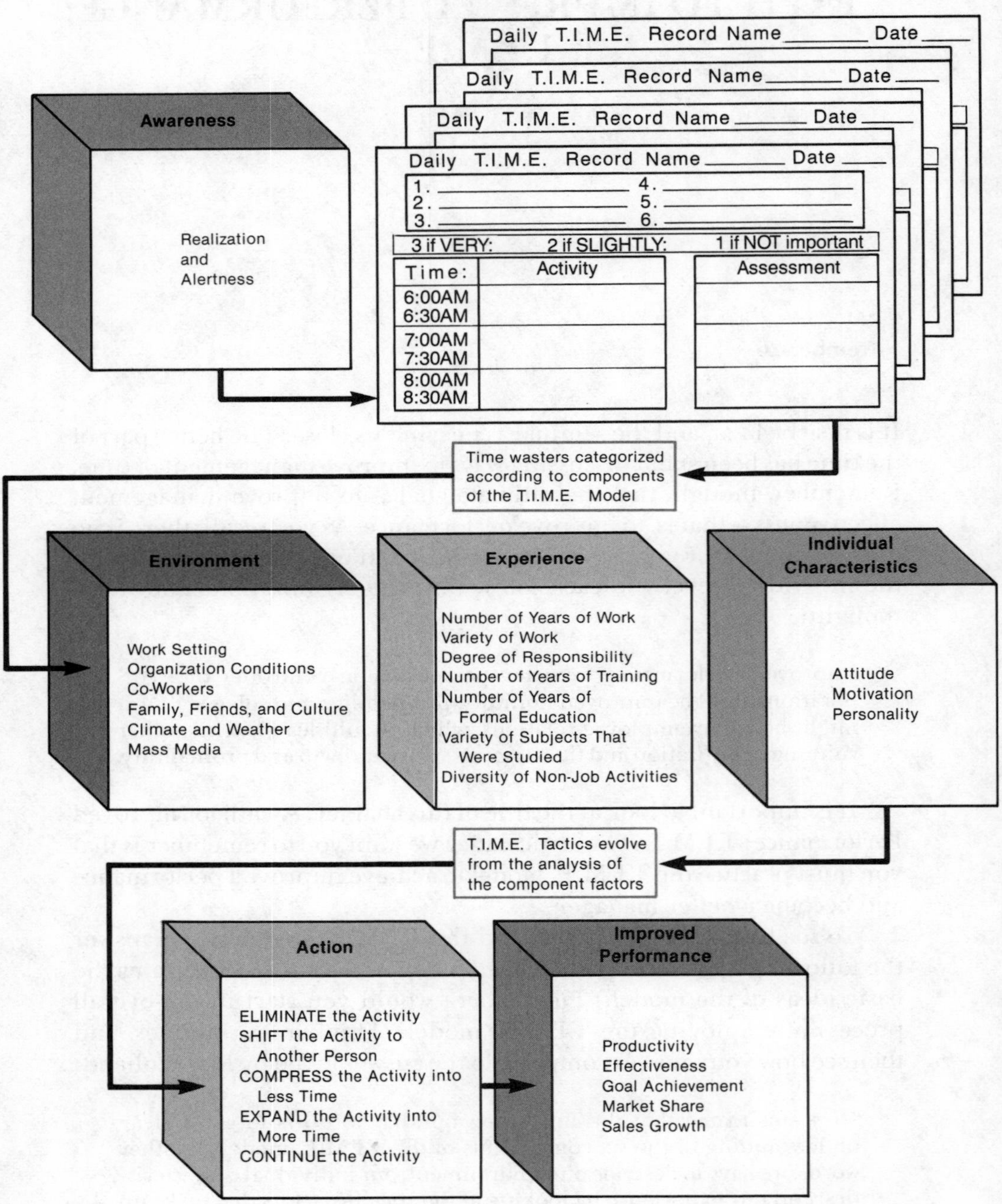
T.I.M.E. Summary
Awareness
Realization and Alertness
Daily T.I.M.E. Record Name ______ Date ______
1. ______ 4. ______
2. ______ 5. ______
3. ______ 6. ______
3 if VERY: 2 if SLIGHTLY: 1 if NOT important
Time: Activity Assessment
6:00AM
6:30AM
7:00AM
7:30AM
8:00AM
8:30AM
Time wasters categorized according to components of the T.I.M.E. Model
Environment
Work Setting
Organization Conditions
Co-Workers
Family, Friends, and Culture
Climate and Weather
Mass Media
Experience
Number of Years of Work
Variety of Work
Degree of Responsibility
Number of Years of Training
Number of Years of Formal Education
Variety of Subjects That Were Studied
Diversity of Non-Job Activities
Individual Characteristics
Attitude
Motivation
Personality
T.I.M.E. Tactics evolve from the analysis of the component factors
Action
ELIMINATE the Activity
SHIFT the Activity to Another Person
COMPRESS the Activity into Less Time
EXPAND the Activity into More Time
CONTINUE the Activity
Improved Performance
Productivity
Effectiveness
Goal Achievement
Market Share
Sales Growth

these components. In addition, I would suggest that we get a working understanding of what we mean by awareness, action, and improved performance. Once we understand the model and how it works, we are in a position to apply the model to our use of time."

The next logical question is What's the next step? Compare your answer to this question to the answer given by Christina Jones:

> "By looking at the diagram and by relating what I understand we have accomplished in this seminar, I would suggest that we become aware of how we use or abuse our time. Awareness evolves by applying the Daily T.I.M.E. Record. This record must be employed by paying attention to specific procedures that have been previously discussed. When you analyze the Daily T.I.M.E. Record, it will provide you with a means of identifying relevant time wasters. The next step is to categorize these time wasters according to the components of the model — that is, using environment, experience, and individual characteristics. The misuses of managerial time can be specifically related to the factors within the components."

Her answer was a good one. We should start by relating time wasters to such factors as years of experience, variety of work, years of training, and so on if the wasters relate to the experience component. Or we would relate them to the work setting, organizational conditions, co-workers, and so forth if they were environmental components, and so on with time wasters that relate to individual characteristics.

What is the next step? Are you thinking along the same lines as Jeff Med?

> "The next step is action. Action would evolve by eliminating, shifting, compressing, extending, or continuing certain types of activities. Specifically, what is required is to transform time wasters into time tactics. Analysis of time wasters, in light of the factors of the components, provides the basis for this positive restructuring. I would suggest the implementation of the T.I.M.E. tactic as the action that brings forth the desired goal — improved performance."

In closing, let us emphasize the key steps: (1) Review the T.I.M.E. model and understand its components and its factors; (2) employ the Daily T.I.M.E. Record to create awareness; (3) identify time wasters; (4) categorize them by using the components of the T.I.M.E. model; (5) restructure T.I.M.E. wasters into T.I.M.E. Tactics by relating the wasters to the factors of the components; (6) implement the T.I.M.E. Tactics, taking the appropriate action. The results should be improved performance.

We urge you to practice the T.I.M.E. model — it is a viable tool to achieve greater job enjoyment and improved management effectiveness.

9
RON HOLLAND ONE YEAR LATER

It had been one year since Ron Holland attended the T.I.M.E. program. He sat back and thought for a moment:

> Over the past year, I actually used the T.I.M.E. model I learned during that seminar. It is an effective mechanism for identifying time wasters and for making improvements. I'm especially happy that my secretary participated in a secretarial development program, and through our joint efforts, we developed a better scheduling system, improved our filing system, and instituted procedures that now screen incoming phone calls.

Some of the activities that Ron engages in, such as the long phone conversations with his friend Eric Mead, were classified as potential time wasters. However, experience has proved to Ron how much he values this relationship, and he is willing to accept the phone calls as a valid use of his time. Ron decided to save time in other ways. All managers will have to determine which activities they value and want to continue and which they wish to execute more efficiently or eliminate.

What did the T.I.M.E. model do for Ron Holland? When he applied the model to his work habits, he found that many of his time wasters were related to his individual characteristics. Some time wasters were personality oriented, and others were attitude oriented. For example, the model prompted him to think about aspects of his environment that could be improved. He realized that his secretary could be used more effectively. By sending her to a time management seminar, he encouraged her motivation to resolve office problems. Ron's new scheduling system was largely her idea, but it wasn't until he communicated the problem to her and then motivated her to present her ideas that the problem was solved.

The T.I.M.E. model helped Ron Holland analyze his personal and environmental characteristics to ascertain which were controllable and thus manageable and which were uncontrollable and thus not worth working on. Through this examination, Ron was able to incorporate four or five new ideas into his work habits that increased his effectiveness. These changes, combined with a more positive attitude at work, have altered his leadership style, and his improved performance is affecting the performance of his entire company. (A review of his company's financial performance shows that both sales and profits are up.)

Ron is now in better control of himself and his schedule than he was before he attended the T.I.M.E. seminar. He has been arriving home earlier and has been able to give more time to his family and other interests. Many of these improvements can be attributed to the fact that he learned a new way of examining himself, his work habits, and his relationships within the company. Through patient, careful examination, motivated by the T.I.M.E. program, he attained insights that he put into practice in his own life and that he shared with his employees. The impact of this momentum was finally fully appreciated one year later. The T.I.M.E. model paid off for Ron Holland, and it can pay off for you.

Bibliography

Forest, Robert B. "Time Gentlemen, Time." *Infosystems,* May 1979, p. 24.

Jackson, John H., and Hayen, Roger L. "Rationing the Scarcest Resource: A Manager's Time." *Personnel Journal,* October 1974, pp. 752–756.

LeBouef, Michael. "Managing Time Means Managing Yourself." *Business Horizons,* February 1980, pp. 41–46.

MacKenzie, R. Alec. *The Time Trap: How To Get More Done in Less Time.* New York: McGraw-Hill, 1975.

May, John W. "How to Use Managerial Time." *Personnel Journal,* May 1978, pp. 213–216.

Mott, Dennis L. "Time Management." In *National Business Education Yearbook.* Reston, VA: National Business Education Association, 1980.

Prestbo, Jon A. "Don't Waste Time." *The Wall Street Journal,* 11 December 1978, p. 22.

Rotenbury, Harry C. "Time Management and Scheduling." *Management World,* March 1979, pp. 27–28.

Settle, Kenneth B. "Time Manages You?" *BSU Journal for Business Educators,* February 1972, pp. 2–7.

Webb, Stan G. "Productivity Through Practical Planning." *Administrative Management,* August 1981, pp. 47–49.

APPENDIX
DAILY T.I.M.E. RECORD FORMS

DAILY T.I.M.E. RECORD

Name ________________ Date ________

Daily Goals:

1. ________________ 4. ________________
2. ________________ 5. ________________
3. ________________ 6. ________________

Evaluate each activity as 3 if VERY important, 2 if SLIGHTLY important, 1 if NOT important

Time	Activity	Assessment
6:00 A.M. 6:30 A.M.		
7:00 A.M. 7:30 A.M.		
8:00 A.M. 8:30 A.M.		

Time	Activity	Assessment
9:00 A.M.		
9:30 A.M.		
10:00 A.M.		
10:30 A.M.		
11:00 A.M.		
11:30 A.M.		
12:00 P.M.		
12:30 P.M.		
1:00 P.M.		
1:30 P.M.		

Time	Activity	Assessment
2:00 P.M.		
2:30 P.M.		
3:00 P.M.		
3:30 P.M.		
4:00 P.M.		
4:30 P.M.		
5:00 P.M.		
5:30 P.M.		
6:00 P.M.		
EVENING		

DAILY T.I.M.E. RECORD

Name ______________ Date ______

Daily Goals:

1. ______________
2. ______________
3. ______________
4. ______________
5. ______________
6. ______________

Evaluate each activity as 3 if VERY important, 2 if SLIGHTLY important, 1 if NOT important

Time	Activity	Assessment
6:00 A.M.		
6:30 A.M.		
7:00 A.M.		
7:30 A.M.		
8:00 A.M.		
8:30 A.M.		

Time	Activity	Assessment
9:00 A.M.		
9:30 A.M.		
10:00 A.M.		
10:30 A.M.		
11:00 A.M.		
11:30 A.M.		
12:00 P.M.		
12:30 P.M.		
1:00 P.M.		
1:30 P.M.		

Time	Activity	Assessment
2:00 P.M. 2:30 P.M.		
3:00 P.M. 3:30 P.M.		
4:00 P.M. 4:30 P.M.		
5:00 P.M. 5:30 P.M.		
6:00 P.M. EVENING